"i DIDN'T SCREAM.
i DIDN'T SHOUT.
JUST: 'RECLAIMING
    MY TIME.'"

RECLAIMING HER TIME

THE POWER OF
MAXINE WATERS

HELENA ANDREWS-DYER AND R. ERIC THOMAS
WITH ILLUSTRATIONS BY SABRINA DORSAINVIL

DEY ST.
An Imprint of WILLIAM MORROW

HarperCollins books may be purchased for educational, business, or sales promotional use. For information, please email the Special Markets Department at SPsales@harpercollins.com.

FIRST EDITION

Designed by Renata De Oliveira
Watercolor backgrounds by KanokpolTokumhnerd/shutterstock

Library of Congress Cataloging-in-Publication Data

Names: Andrews-Dyer, Helena, author. | Thomas, R. Eric, author. | Dorsainvil, Sabrina, illustrator.
Title: Reclaiming her time : the life, wit, and wisdom of American icon Maxine Waters / Helena Andrews-Dyer and R. Eric Thomas; with illustrations by Sabrina Dorsainvil.
Description: First edition. | New York : Dey Street, [2020] | Includes bibliographical references and index. | Summary: "In the tradition of Notorious RBG, a lively, beautifully designed, full-color illustrated celebration of the life, wisdom, wit, legacy, and fearless style of iconic American Congresswoman Maxine Waters. "Let me just say this: I'm a strong black woman, and I cannot be intimidated. I cannot be undermined. I cannot be thought to be afraid of Bill O'Reilly or anyone."-Maxine Waters To millions nationwide, Congresswoman Maxine Waters is a hero of the resistance and an icon, serving eye rolls, withering looks, and sharp retorts to any who dare waste her time on nonsense. But behind the Auntie Maxine meme is a seasoned public servant and she's not here to play. Throughout her forty years in public service and eighty years on earth, U.S. Representative for California's 43rd district has been a role model, a crusader for justice, a game-changer, a trailblazer, and an advocate for the marginalized who has long defied her critics, including her most vocal detractor, Donald J. Trump. And she's just getting started. From her anti-apartheid work and support of affirmative action to her passionate opposition to the Iraq War and calls to hold Trump to account, you can count on Auntie Maxine to speak truth to power and do it with grace and, sometimes, sass. As ranking member of the House Financial Services Committee and one of the most powerful black women in America, she is the strong, ethical voice the country has always needed, especially right now. Reclaiming Her Time pays tribute to all things Maxine Waters, from growing up in St. Louis "too skinny" and "too black," to taking on Wall Street during the financial crisis and coming out on top in her legendary showdowns with Trump and his cronies. Featuring inspiring highlights from her personal life and political career, beloved memes, and testimonies from her many friends and fans, Reclaiming Her Time is a funny, warm, and admiring portrait of a champion who refuses to stay silent in the face of corruption and injustice; a powerful woman who is an inspiration to us all."—Provided by publisher.
Identifiers: LCCN 2020008250 | ISBN 9780062992031 (hardcover) | ISBN 9780062992048 (ebook)
Subjects: LCSH: Waters, Maxine—Influence. | United States. Congress. House—Biography. | Women legislators—United States—Biography. | Legislators—United States—Biography. | African American women legislators—United States—Biography. | African American women legislators—California—Los Angeles—Biography. | Legislators—California—Los Angeles—Biography.
Classification: LCC E901.1.W38 A74 2020 | DDC 973.933092 [B]—dc23
LC record available at https://lccn.loc.gov/2020008250

ISBN 978-0-06-299203-1

20 21 22 23 24 LSC 10 9 8 7 6 5 4 3 2 1

FOR ANYONE WHO WAS TOLD

THEY WERE TOO MUCH—TOO BLACK,

TOO SKINNY, TOO LOUD, TOO SMART,

TOO STRONG, TOO IN-YOUR-FACE.

TURNS OUT, YOU ARE JUST ENOUGH.

CONTENTS

MAXINE WATERS
CONGRESSWOMAN

FEARLESS LEADER FOR AMERICA

INTRODUCTION

"I'M HAVING THE TIME OF MY LIFE
WITH THE MILLENNIALS."

There are people squeezed into every available nook and cranny in the K Street bookstore and more performance venue Busboys and Poets. They have spread out all over the main room, overflowed the side room with VIP access, and lined up on the spiral staircase like Von Trapp children, and more are pushing against the glass doors trying to get in. They are hype, tweeting about their location, taking shots for Insta, murmuring excitedly. Most have come from the surrounding area and a few from far-flung destinations; they brought tote bags and T-shirts with the same name on them; they clamor for the buttons that are being given away bearing an iconic face with an iconic expression: red "readers," pulled down to reveal an imperious stare. Then the person they've been waiting for finally emerges, makes her way through the crowd, takes the stage, and declares, "We're gonna *stop* his ass!" and the room bursts into rock-concert-level mania. But the crowd that has gathered here in mid-April 2017 isn't swooning over a *Billboard*-topping recording artist or the star of the latest Marvel movie. The person they came to see is, improbably, a seventy-eight-year-old congresswoman from California.

Maxine Waters is not a celebrity. At least, not in the sense that we usually think of celebrity. Yes, a Maxine reaction GIF—of which there are plenty—will win any argument; yes, you've seen her on everything from *The View* to MTV, presenting, Tracee Ellis Ross, yes, there is a wide world of Maxine paraphernalia, from shirts to notebooks to bobbleheads to prayer candles. And no, this is not typical for most politicians. But Maxine Waters, you already know, is not your typi-

" I FOUND OUT THAT PEOPLE LOVE ME TO SAY IT. AND IT'S SOMETHING THAT THEY WANT TO SAY, OR THEY'VE BEEN THINKING, BUT THEY JUST NEVER HAD THE COURAGE TO SAY IT. "

cal politician. In the game for more than forty years, she has more receipts than a CVS; she's had rousing political successes every decade of her career; she is well respected and accomplished; and, on this spring day in Busboys and Poets, she is using a moment of viral fame to galvanize a new generation of voters and activists. Though the circumstances of the moment are new to her, the impetus behind them—motivating everyday citizens to act, speaking truth to power, and stopping his ass (whomever the dastardly ass in question belongs to)—has been part of her work from day one. On this night, she's successfully drumming up support for a rally she'll hold the next day to raise awareness about Donald Trump's heretofore unreleased tax returns. She's flown in that day from Los Angeles, where she had another rally, and will end up being at Busboys and Poets until well after 10 P.M. *And* she has laryngitis. Maybe she *is* one of those Marvel superheroes after all.

How did all of this begin? Well, in one view it began with an ad for a Head Start teacher that she answered in the mid-1970s. In another view, it started in the 1990s when she struck a defiant figure, speaking up for the residents of her district during the Los Angeles uprising. Or perhaps it started the day she was assigned to the House Financial Services Committee in 2013, the first step on her road to becoming one of the most powerful politicians (black, female, or otherwise). Or maybe it was in 1992, when she strode into a closed-door meeting held by President George H. W. Bush despite not being invited. Or . . . well, you get the picture. This may be Maxine's moment, but you'd be hard-pressed to find a time that wasn't hers also. All time belongs to Maxine Waters, reclaimed or not. She's known for her brilliant ability to work behind the scenes to get things done, her dogged commitment to her constituents, her flashy style, and, of course, her way with words. And it's perhaps this last component that has so captivated her newest fans, after a succession of spicy public statements after the election of Donald Trump raised the congresswoman's profile and endeared her to millions. "I do say outrageous things sometimes," she conceded with a smile and a small shrug during an interview with Eric. "I found out that people love me to say it. And it's something that they want to say, or they've been thinking about, but they just never had the courage to say it." Maxine Waters has always had the courage.

Consider this moment from early 2017, a moment that arguably launched the Modern Maxine Era. It was January 13 in the year of our Lord 2017 when Maxine Waters—legislator, legend—had had enough. She'd just walked out of a classified briefing on the Russia investigation and the press was waiting with questions. Podiums and microphones usually mean press conference, but on this day those silly things were just in the way of Maxine's next appointment. Dressed to represent in a black pencil skirt, slingbacks, and red lips, she kicked off the conference like an impatient bank teller who knows you know she knows you're in overdraft. "Yes? Can I help you? What do you want?" she asked the gathered reporters like they were trick-or-treaters who showed up on November 1. She then took but two questions from reporters before declaring, with frustration, "The FBI director has *no* credibility!"

Then she exited stage left down a marble hallway, her heels clickety-clacking, her hand waving along the silent men trailing in her wake. It was, in a word, a moment. A Maxine moment. One of many that have flourished since 2016, when the man she says is the worst she's ever seen got elected president. This was the Maxine Waters the kids were talking about. But that moment in January 2017 wasn't manufactured by consultants with a large marketing budget— nor was it a fluke. *Maybe she was just hangry that day?* No, that press conference is what happens when a lifetime (yes, fifty years) of public service and a habit of frequently, vociferously speaking one's mind collide in the social media swamp of the twenty-first century, boosted by a reality show president and a divided nation. It's also just another day's work for Congresswoman Waters, who stays ready, willing, and able to strap this country to her back and carry it to a better, truer, and more just place.

Since Trump's unlikely election, the memes weren't just born, they were deployed. They were like an army of virtual resistance soldiers occupying Twitter, Instagram, and Facebook as proof positive there was someone on the Hill who felt the same about official Washington—*this ish is crazy!*—as you did. Suddenly the congresswoman had become a media darling and millennial rock star. Sharon Stone (yep) performed a spoken word poem for her via YouTube. There was a "Reclaiming My Time" gospel mash-up. There were the frequent appearances on *All In with Chris Hayes* that routinely blew the host's hair back. She was dubbed "Auntie Maxine," a nickname that seemed to call to mind her take-no-prisoners approach and her razor-sharp wit, like your favorite relative at the cookout. "Auntie" Maxine Waters got so big so fast, it may have seemed like an overnight sensation. "Seemed" being the operative word there.

Waters holds a shirt with her image and catchphrase made by Nineteenth Amendment clothing.

Life-giving as they were, those Maxine moments were but reminders of a long career that brought Waters from humble beginnings as a Head Start teacher in the projects to meetings with Nelson Mandela and Hillary Clinton and Barack Obama. With multiple generations of voters now privy to Maxine's brand of no-bullshit governance, it's as if she's had to reintroduce herself. *Yes? Can I help you? What do you want?* This moment isn't the redefinition of Maxine Waters, because homegirl ain't changed. Waters has been a public servant since 1966. She has nearly fifty years of community activism, Los Angeles City Hall management, California State House success, and congressional accomplishments to sear your eyebrows on her CV. She's not new to this, she's true to this.

So, dear reader, before we truly begin, before we peel back the curtain on the Maxine Show, first we must get one thing straight: Congresswoman Waters—the eighty-one-year-old with more political power in her pinkie finger than Kellyanne Conway has in her entire body—is not, in fact, your auntie.

Oh, you might recognize an auntie's no-nonsense pragmatism in Maxine's bone-chilling over-her-glasses up-and-down glare. You might be all too familiar with her exasperated sighs and storm-out-of-the-press-conference stomps from your last family reunion. But to be clear, Maxine Waters is nobody's sweeps-week special guest star. She is a force, a superhero, a major pain in President Trump's ass, and a standard bearer for anyone who just wanted to say, "Screw this," and blow out the door of a boring meeting that was going nowhere. She is what the country needs right now, and she's been what this country has needed for more than forty years of public service.

In short, she was, is, and forever will be a real one. That's who we are fascinated by. The real woman.

What we will do in these pages is show just how real Maxine Waters truly is. We immersed ourselves deep into Waters's own words (including an interview by Eric, one of her faves, conducted in her office), scoured newspaper archives and her legislative record, and interviewed folks who knew her way back when—all in an effort to paint a three-dimensional picture of the congresswoman. Too often, black women are drawn in flat lines. They pop up in plotlines to make us feel smart and important or sassy. What Maxine makes us feel is truly seen. She is familiar, like looking into a mirror. We think that's where the rush to name her kinfolk comes from. The warm feeling that this woman talking triple truth to power is like us. Well, she is and she isn't. Because while Maxine Waters is wholly herself and has been from jump, at times she can seem almost unreal—too good, too unintentionally hilarious, too spot-on for the moment. Therein lies her power, forever walking the line between relatable and magical. This book will shed light on the woman behind the finger snaps and novelty T-shirts. The woman who despite being picked apart time and time again, having to not only reclaim her time but prove her worth, still gets up every morning at the crack of dawn to do the work.

Waters in 2017.

Born in 1938, "too skinny" and "too black," Waters went from welfare to taking on Wall Street—by being relentless. This is the story of how the little girl born fifth of thirteen children to a mother struggling to make ends meet became the woman who would capture the national imagination, inspire memes and slogans, and turn the tide of history. This is the story of a black woman who set out to lead a life of public service and found herself elevated to iconic status. This is the story of an American who would not sit idly by while her rights and her country were being trampled. This book captures the life and (reclaimed) times of an extraordinary woman from ordinary beginnings and the country she went to bat for.

This is Maxine Waters's time; we're just lucky to live in it.

CHAPTER ONE

THE MEME

JULY 27, 2017

IN WHICH THE GENTLE LADY
FROM CALIFORNIA BECOMES
THE INTERNET'S IT GIRL

she wasn't the first to say it. "Reclaiming my time," the three words that launched Maxine Waters into the millennial meme stratosphere, is, in fact, a pretty common expression on Capitol Hill. It's formal phraseology that has been used on the House floor and in congressional committee meetings and hearings for decades. *Excuse me, hi, thank you, stop talking, right now, please.* "Reclaiming my time" is a major key in the legislative lexicon. Do a quick search on C-SPAN and you'll find thousands, literally thousands, of examples starring the men and women who make our laws politely giving one another a verbal tap on the shoulder. You know what the difference is between Maxine Waters and all those other members? She makes it sound *good*.

For anyone unfamiliar (who are you people?), this is *the* Maxine moment (one of many we'll discuss in this book) that reintroduced the not-so-gentle lady from California to kids today. More than her blunt assessments of President Trump, James Comey, and another dude who didn't live up to her high standards, the congresswoman's takedown of Steve Mnuchin counts as Peak Maxine and as such deserves a thorough examination.

It was Thursday, July 27, 2017, when newly minted secretary of the Treasury, executive producer of *The Lego Movie* Steve Mnuchin, showed up to a House Financial Services Committee meeting fully prepared to testify about the intricacies of the international finance system. What he wasn't prepared for, however, was a run-in with then ranking member Maxine Waters, who showed up to work dressed to interrogate in a string of pearls and a red lip—all the better to eat you alive with, sir.

At issue for Congresswoman Waters, the senior Democrat on the committee, was an official letter she and her party colleagues sent Mnuchin's office that had, as of their July face-to-face, still gone unanswered. Unacceptable. In the letter, Maxine and friends wanted to know more about President Trump's financial ties to Russia. She didn't like being ghosted. This is how it all went down, emphasis our own:

WATERS [NOT HERE TO PLAY]: Is there some reason why I did not get a response to the letter that I sent May 23rd?

MNUCHIN [PLAYING]: So, Ranking Member Waters, first of all let me thank you for your service to California. Being a resident of California I appreciate everything that you've done for the community there. I also have appreciated the opportunity to meet with you several times—

WATERS [ALREADY OVER IT]: Reclaiming my time. Reclaiming my time.

CHAIR OF FINANCIAL SERVICES REPRESENTATIVE JEB HENSARLING: The time belongs to the gentle lady from California.

WATERS: Let me just say to you, thank you for your compliments about how great I am, but I don't want to waste my time on me. I want to know about the May 23rd letter. You know about it. Why did you not respond to me and my colleagues?

MNUCHIN: I was going to answer that.

WATERS: Just please go straight to the answer.

MNUCHIN [IN SEARCH OF SOLIDARITY]: Mr. Chairman, I thought when you read the rules you acknowledged that I shouldn't be interrupted and that I would have the oppor—

WATERS [ALL OUT OF F--KS]: Reclaiming my time. What he failed to tell you was when you're on my time I can reclaim it. He left that out so I'm reclaiming my time. Please will you respond to the question of why I did not get a response, me and my colleagues, to the May 23rd letter?

MNUCHIN: Well, I was going to tell you my response.

WATERS: Just tell me.

MNUCHIN: Okay, so first of all, okay, let me just say that the Department of Treasury has cooperated extensively with the Senate Intel Committee, with the House Intel Committ—

WATERS: Reclaiming my time.

MNUCHIN: —with the Senate Judiciary Committ—

WATERS: Reclaiming my time.

MNUCHIN: Matter of fa—

WATERS: Reclaiming my time.

HENSARLING: Mr. Secretary, the time belongs to the gentle lady from California.

MNUCHIN [OUT OF OPTIONS]: Perhaps, Mr. Chairman, I don't understand the rules because I thought I was allowed to answer questions.

WATERS: Reclaiming my time. Would you please explain the rules and do not take that away from my time.

HENSARLING: We will give the gentle lady adequate time. So, what I read, Mr. Secretary, were statements of the ranking member and Democrat [*sic*] colleagues on how administration witnesses *should* be treated, not necessarily the way they *will* be treated. So, the time belongs to the gentle lady from California, but I assure you majority members will allow you to answer the question when it is *our* time.

MNUCHIN: So, uh, what I was saying is that we have provided substantial information. We believe there's significant overlap. . . .

And the wonkiness continued with a chastened Mnuchin no longer trying to grasp for nonexistent straws and instead answering Waters's questions with a quickness. In effect, homeboy got schooled. The Internet, of course, took that moment and ran with it. A better scene couldn't have been written for the movie *Trump-Tales: Woo-Noo,* and no two people could have been better cast for the roles of Powerful Black Boss and Boring White Coworker. Here was a black woman of mature age and experience refusing to give this white man, so new to his job his parking pass was probably still being printed, an inch. "Reclaiming my time"? Who knew parliamentary rules threw so much shade? This is what the Congressional Research Service, the Library of Congress's public policy think tank for the House and Senate, says about the management of "time" among members:

> *[Any] Member who has been recognized in debate may "yield to" another Member for a question or comment. When one Member yields to another, the yielding Member retains the floor and should remain standing. Any time consumed by the Member yielded to is charged against the portion of time yielded originally by the manager to the Member who has been recognized. For this reason, Members ask permission to use another Member's time. If a Member wants to interrupt another Member to ask a question or respond to something that was said, he or she can ask the presiding officer: Will the gentleman (or gentlewoman) yield?*
>
> *The Member speaking can decline to yield. Or, the Member can respond:*
>
> *I yield to the gentleman (or gentlewoman).*
>
> *The time being consumed belongs to the Member who yielded. Therefore, the Member who was yielded to cannot yield to a third Member. If another Member wants to join the discussion between the yielding Member and the Member who was yielded to, he or she would have to seek permission to interrupt from the yielding Member. These practices of*

yielding permit Members to engage in a colloquy, with one
Member yielding to one or more Members in turn so that they
may exchange information or debate an issue. Furthermore,
the Member who has yielded to another Member can take
the time back. Generally, this is done by interrupting the
Member who had been yielded to by saying:
Reclaiming my time. . . .

In English? We turned to Donald Garrett, a millennial *and* professional parliamentarian (they do exist), to break it down so that it will forever and consistently be broke. This is the duh moment: "If everyone was shouting at the same time that wouldn't help," Garrett told us. "Each person has their own time." Basically, during a House floor debate (or committee hearing or meeting), the chair recognizes a member for five minutes. Those three hundred seconds are priceless, and each individual member is in control of how her time is used. At a hearing after the member poses a question, she yields her precious time to the witness for answers—allegedly. So, the clock is ticking. If the witness is rambling (read: going on and on about how great she is) or doing anything else but answering said question, the member can say, "Reclaiming my time," and the witness is supposed to shut up, er, stop speaking.

Similarly, this time ownership manual also applies when two members of the committee are interacting. If Member A is recognized and for whatever reason Member B double Dutches into Member A's five minutes, Member A can "reclaim her time" if Member B is ball hogging. That is why when Waters instructed Chairman Hensarling to take a pause for the cause and explain to Secretary Mnuchin how this whole thing worked, the congresswoman made clear to add, "And do not take that away from my time." To some it sounded rude AF, but it wasn't. It was completely within her rights.

It was also Exhibit 1619 of black women looking angry when really they're just out there living their lives.

"Maxine Waters has been doing this for decades. It looks nasty, but from a technical perspective that's exactly what you say to stop the clock for the witness," added Garrett. "It took on a dual meaning, but it was very technically correct."

Why all the technicalities and formalities? Because members of Congress are supposed to be treating one another with respect, and the only way to get folks to do that is to make them speak like Cookie Monster. At least that's how Garrett, twenty-seven, a professional parliamentarian in his spare time, explained it.

"The idea behind speaking in the third person, directing remarks through the chairman, calling people 'gentleman' and 'gentle lady,' etc., is to make the debate more impersonal. It helps to cool tensions during spicy meetings," said Garrett. "For example, it is much easier to yell out 'You are a liar!' compared to 'I believe the gentleman from Virginia needs to reexamine the facts.' Or 'Shut up, I'm speaking' compared to 'Reclaiming my time.'

"The idea is for members to speak in an esteemed manner so that meetings don't break down," added Garrett, who has been obsessed with *Robert's Rules of Order* since high school and for whom Maxine Waters's "reclaiming my time" hit single was something of a "dream come true" (his words). It's not every day that parliamentary procedure and pop culture get married and make a viral baby.

All this is important to understand because the Auntie Maxine character was born out of that exchange with Mnuchin, an exchange that, sure, sounded sassy and resistance-y but was, in the end, completely routine when you look at it. The woman was just doing her job.

The congresswoman herself was originally taken aback by the fuss.

"Yeah, that surprised me. Because I didn't create it," she said in a *Washington Post Magazine* interview. "That is the regular order of business to get your time back after it's been imposed on by your witness. So, members have used that; I wasn't the first."

Not the first but definitely the one with the most finesse. It wasn't just what Maxine said but *how* she said it and *whom* she said it to. If you listen closely, Waters's voice throughout the exchange vacillates between exasperated schoolteacher just trying to understand why her first grader won't stop eating paste to intense prosecutor circling

Waters in 2019.

for the aha moment. With decades of parliamentary procedure under her belt, Waters is a guru when it comes to expressing her full self within the rules. That's a feat—coloring yourself inside the lines without losing an inch. Therein lies the magic of the "reclaiming my time" instant. Maxine Waters was Maxine Waters in a place where folks (those who didn't know her, obviously) expected her to be someone else. Perhaps someone less blunt and more polite, someone less powerful and more palatable. Maxine Waters does not play small.

Take, for example, Waters's run-in with Mnuchin nearly two years after the congresswoman made "reclaiming my time" happen. In April 2019, the Treasury secretary once again found himself at a House Financial Services Committee hearing, but this time he was dealing with Chairwoman Waters, who'd been bumped up from ranking member when the Democrats swept the House in 2018. And once again the two public servants were arguing over time. After three hours in the witness chair, Mnuchin, doing his best impression of the White Rabbit in *Alice in Wonderland,* was late for a very important date! "I have a foreign leader waiting in my office at 5:30. . . . I hope you understand I'm already going to be late," he told Waters, who had asked that he stay for an additional fifteen minutes so that everyone on the committee could get their questions in.

"We're all late all the time, unfortunately," Waters said. "We're all pressed for time, and I do get it." She got it, but that didn't change the facts. She wanted him to stay and he wanted to go. The two played tug-of-war over the clock for some time. It appeared as if the congresswoman would yield when she told the secretary, "You are

Three-year-old Arya George dresses as Representative Waters for Halloween.

free to leave any time you want." But Mnuchin, sensing the trap, asked for Waters to officially adjourn the hearing. "Please dismiss everybody," he said. "I believe you are supposed to take the gravel [*sic*] and bang it." Bless his heart.

"Please do not instruct me as to how I am to conduct this committee," said Maxine. The look on her face, child. Sleepy children the world over sat up straight in church. In the end, Mnuchin stayed for those extra fifteen minutes he spent three minutes arguing about and he even agreed to come back at a later date.

The congresswoman had her own theory as to why her initial exchange with Mnuchin took off: mainly, she said, because of President Trump and what his cabinet members represented—an election stolen, mediocrity celebrated, and real damage to our democracy. So, from the start, she was held up as a resistance forerunner by her mere presence. And what a presence it was. "And I think that," she told *The Washington Post Magazine*, "when [I had] Mnuchin in front of me, here is this African American woman who was being forceful. Because I didn't say it one time. I said it several times, you know. I didn't scream. I didn't shout. Just: 'Reclaiming my time.' And it caught on."

She didn't scream and she didn't shout because she didn't have to. Throughout her career Maxine Waters has remained even-keeled and consistent no matter the decade. She is not trendy, she is transcendent. The fact that she became famous by doing what she's always done is a testament to not only her staying power but also her particular superpower—bending time to her will. (Remember when she was the only one calling for President Trump's impeachment and folks were calling *her* crazy? How'd that whole thing turn out?)

Time. Is it a line, a circle, or a social construct? Who knows? But for Maxine Waters it is a lightning rod and a wand. She's weaponized it, in this her not-so-twilight years of service. Time is what makes the gentle lady from California stand out from everyone else. She's walking around with loads of it in her back pocket and somehow it hasn't seemed to wear her down. Her former staffers call her the "Energizer bunny," a member who rarely gets tired (at least not in public). All time belongs to Maxine Waters, because instead of wrestling with it, she leans into it. In the 1960s she responded to civil unrest in Watts by becoming a community organizer, in the 1970s she answered the call of the women's movement and ran for office, in the 1980s she set out to dismantle structural racism by fighting for South African divestment, and in the 1990s she owned the anger of South Central Los Angeles after the Rodney King verdict. She's embraced hip-hop, endorsed Bill Clinton, rejected Donald Trump, and done so much else in between.

> "I DIDN'T SCREAM. I DIDN'T SHOUT. JUST: 'RECLAIMING MY TIME!'"

Maxine Waters is both a student of time and its spiritual guide. She reclaims it, wields it, and outruns it. That could be why that moment with Mnuchin went so viral. It was like watching a conductor direct her master symphony, a culmination of decades of learning that looks as simple as a flick of the wrist. Or in Maxine's case, an expertly arched eyebrow.

CHAPTER TWO

MAXINE IN THE MAKING

1938–1965

IN WHICH OUR SUBJECT JOURNEYS
FROM ST. LOUIS TO SOUTH CENTRAL
LOS ANGELES AND FINDS HER CALLING

I t's hard to picture Maxine Waters as a little girl. It shouldn't be, but it is, right? It's often difficult to dream up heroes, idols, warriors, your faves in anything other than full-on color, as any ounce less than grandiose. But every Superwoman has a mythical origin story; every badass butterfly was once just inching its way through the dirt toward greatness. *Wait, wait, you mean to tell me there's a version of* the *Maxine Waters in the space-time continuum who goo-goo and gaagaa'd? Who didn't know how to talk, much less talk back? Like she didn't just spring from Zeus's head fully grown and ready to eff things up like Athena?* Well, yes and no. It appears as if the future congresswoman known for winning fights may have been born for the task. Cliché, we know. But that doesn't make it any less true. For better or worse, little Maxine Carr was forced to stand up for herself straight out the gate.

"[I was] the first in my family to come out too skinny, too black, and too looking like they say my father looked," Waters recalled in an interview. Her mother, Velma Lee, married her father, Remus Carr Sr., in the early 1930s. Velma was a teenager at the time. Born in a tiny Mississippi Delta town called Cotton Plant, Arkansas, in 1916, Velma traveled upriver in search of not just new but *any* opportunity. On August 15, 1938, Velma, twenty-two, gave birth to her fifth child and fourth girl, Maxine. She was a dead ringer for Remus, who didn't stick around past Maxine's second birthday. After he left Velma and kids, Maxine could recall seeing Remus only once more a few years later, and then never again. She barely remembered him. Eventually, Velma would remarry, this time to Samuel Moore. But Remus's memory was impossible to shake with Maxine, his mini-me, underfoot. Even as she grew, the little girl looked just like him—everyone said so. Perhaps it was those same high and diamond-cut cheekbones. Those same sparkling eyes. Velma and

Maxine bumped heads because of the resemblance, the ever-present painful reminder. "If my father was someone who had gotten himself together, fine, but he had not done what he should do—and I was a constant reminder of it."

Can you imagine? Being the equivalent of a walking Facebook memory of the father your mother would rather forget? Of a possibility that popped like a balloon? In the end, the man Velma had pinned her dreams to, the one she had five children with, had disappointed her, and instead of erasing his history she was forced to reckon with it every day in the form of her daughter. It wasn't long before young Maxine developed thick skin and sharp elbows. The unavoidable circumstance was one of her earliest lessons—be better than what folks think you can be. Eventually, Velma's second husband, Sam, would leave her, too. So she was left to raise a baker's dozen—Velma, Rema, Willa, Remus, Maxine, Joseph, Wadsworth, Samella, Kimberly, Sharon, Adrian, Reginald, and Raye—on her own. Poor and with few options, the family found themselves on and off welfare throughout Maxine's childhood.

There are two words Maxine uses to describe her mother: "strong" and "survivor." "She did not raise us with the kind of subtleties that, I suppose, oftentimes parents raise their children with," Waters mused in a *Huffington Post* interview. "They don't want them to get into trouble, they want them to be mindful of whatever they say, they want them to be quiet even when they have an opinion because having that opinion may get you in trouble. I didn't have that." What she had was a house filled with brothers and sisters clawing for room, competing against one another for both the basics and the big things. The thirteen of them were either vying for Velma's attention or arguing about "who was going to wear what clothes and when." Rule one of living in the Carr-Moore household was a simple southern axiom: Closed mouths don't get fed. Speaking up for yourself was a vital requirement, and Velma insisted that all her children learn how to stand up for themselves. She wasn't necessarily loving, overly kind, or even always available—how could she be, raising thirteen children on her own? But what Maxine's mother may have lacked in hugs and kisses, she made up for in sheer force of will.

"She had no filters, really, so I think that most of her children grew up that way. We didn't know that we were speaking out, we didn't know that that was different from the way that other people are taught to react to other people, and to voice their opinion. It was quite natural for us," Maxine explained in an interview with Janet Mock.

Velma, whom everyone called "Ma Dear," was a woman who, without a high school diploma or a partner to rely on, weathered the Great Depression and got it done. The family would stay together, and they would survive. That was one of the other major lessons young Maxine would hold close from St. Louis to Capitol Hill—one of endurance, strength, and fortitude. "She was not an educated woman," Maxine has said of Velma, "but she was a woman of wisdom. And so, she helped to teach us what strength is all about. Standing up for yourself. Being willing to fight for what you think is right."

The neighborhood where Maxine and her siblings grew up was packed on both sides of the street with women like Velma. Women who worked the miracle of making it in a deeply segregated city with few opportunities. Women, who like her mother, didn't have the option of giving up. "I think probably the most important thing that happened in my life," the congresswoman recalled, "was strong African American women who had courage, who got up every day knowing that they had to make something happen. Knowing that they had to provide for their families." The men, plenty of whom got up to work at the Scullin Steel or Armour meatpacking plant early every morning and came home after clocking out, don't loom nearly as large in Maxine's childhood memories as the women.

Working class, intimate, and tight knit, Montrose Avenue was an eight-block stretch near the center of St. Louis in what was a predominantly African American neighborhood known as Mill Creek Valley, a historic community that was razed in the late 1950s in the name of urban renewal. That was the street Maxine, who would be shuffled in and out of St. Louis housing projects as a child, remembers as home. The place that truly raised her. She said, "I remember Montrose because the families on Montrose all knew each other very well. . . . Everybody had big families on Montrose and in that community. Mothers were home having babies, trying to figure out how to feed those children, washing clothes, hanging curtains, scrubbing floors." Waters remembers it as a sort of working-class utopia, describing it as "a little town" where everybody knew everybody. No one locked their doors. Neighbors simply bounced from one house to the next, grabbing a bite to eat, helping with the washing or with

"WHEN YOU HAVE **SELF-ESTEEM,** YOU WILL NOT ALLOW ANYBODY TO RELEGATE YOU TO **POVERTY** OR **MISERY** OR **UNHAPPINESS.**"

the baby, or just dropping by to gossip. In the summertime, folks sat out on their porches and stoops until late in the evening. Nobody could afford air-conditioning and it was too hot to sleep.

On the blocks Maxine called home, life was an interconnected thing, something you conquered or succumbed to together. Folks didn't simply wave hi and bye, disappearing inside their homes to deal with the day alone; they truly knew and cared for one another. So, secrets had nowhere to go on those blocks. Everyone's business was "out on the street." You knew whose husband was a drunk, whose was spending all his money on other women, whose was prone to coming home with his fists clenched on Saturday night and got threatened with a pot of boiling water sprinkled with sugar (so it'd be hot *and* sticky) if he ever tried that crap again.

Poverty is often described as something one must "face." In that sense it is an enemy, a foe to contend with. For Maxine, poverty was simply a fact of life, but it didn't define her. She would not succumb to it, of that much she was sure. "I was never ashamed of it," she said of being on welfare, "but I knew that it was not enough. Being almost a ward of the state in the sense of looking to someone for money to live on was not a quality way to live. I wanted more than that." Somehow Waters knew that she wasn't trapped, and that while the tiny place she grew up was meaningful, it was hardly her last stop. "I never felt helpless or like a victim," she said, remembering her life as a child. How was it that a poor little black girl—the actual embodiment of that tired cliché—could shrug off the societal constraints that would weigh anyone else down? "I have come to believe that until one learns to love and respect oneself, one will not be able to control one's life and destiny," she told *Ebony* magazine in a story about beating welfare. "When you have self-esteem, you will not allow anybody to relegate you to poverty or misery or unhappiness."

As a child, Waters witnessed enough misery and unhappiness to sink a soul. While the industrious women of Montrose Avenue were her earliest teachers—her first heroes—young Maxine knew even then that there was something missing. Because while those courageous women laughed and ruled and wholly owned themselves in the boundaries of the eight blocks that made up her childhood world, Maxine could see how truly confined they were. How boxed in their circumstances made their lives. "They were sad," she recalled, "not because they told you how sad they were, they were sad because you could see it in their eyes. Based on the lifestyle." Despite the hardship that defined much of life inside and outside her home, Maxine was determined to carve out a different path from the one that led the strong women she looked up to to their own disappointments.

Velma, who had a sixth-grade education and spent most of her life working odd jobs or depending on government assistance, was a prime example. "My mother was basically a very hardworking woman. She was not someone who was mean or who tried to hurt anybody," Maxine recalled carefully, with an understanding of her mother's assets and her limitations. Velma was simply trying to per-

"I HAVE COME TO BELIEVE THAT UNTIL ONE LEARNS TO LOVE & RESPECT ONESELF, ONE WILL NOT BE ABLE TO CONTROL ONE'S LIFE & DESTINY."

sist like so many of the women around her. But constantly struggling to keep your head above water doesn't leave a ton of room to breathe and even less to offer a tiny shotgun house filled to the brim with children. "[My mother] didn't always understand the needs of her children, necessarily," Maxine recalled about growing up in Velma's house. "She *often* didn't understand me."

Misunderstood at home, and often overlooked in a sea of siblings, Maxine went about getting noticed. "Just getting *heard* in a family that size is difficult," Waters explained. "We had to scramble for basic things—for space. . . . I had to find my own way." She went searching for that space and the spotlight found her. The Vashon Community Center on Market Street, one of only a few public recreation centers available to African Americans in segregated St. Louis, afforded young Maxine a place to call her own. You could find Maxine there almost every evening after school and most days during the summer months. "This is just amazing when I think about it," Maxine recalled about the time she spent at the rec center, where she learned the graceful movements of ballet, the powerful strokes of competitive swimming, the speed of a track star in the fifty-yard dash, and the skills to play nearly every sport with a ball. She thrived.

School also became Maxine's sanctuary, specifically the teachers who didn't just clock in but who poured themselves into the little girl who sometimes showed up with her braids a bit fuzzy and in clothes a few sizes too big. They fed her when she was hungry and spanked her (it was the 1940s) when she stepped out of line. One even let Maxine come over after school let out to give her (and Velma) some breathing room. Another taught her to play the piano. "We had teachers who cared about you," Maxine remembered in an interview, "and they told you you could do things." Like the blocks of Montrose Avenue, James Weldon Johnson Elementary School on the corner of Lacede and Ewing in St. Louis sat on hallowed ground for Maxine. Two black women who taught in that modest three-story brown building would forever change her, achieving hero status in the eyes of the future congresswoman.

Louise Carter taught fifth-grade math at James Weldon Johnson. Waters describes Carter as "loving." She was the kind of teacher who considered it her job to teach both in and outside of the classroom. Like most of the instructors at the school, Carter lived in the neighborhood and, like everyone else, she knew that Maxine was one of thirteen kids being raised by a single mother. The teachers at James Weldon Johnson often dropped in on their students at home after school and on the weekends. On one such Saturday, Carter had a school picnic planned for her class. When she arrived at the Carr-Moore house to pick up Maxine, the little girl wasn't ready. Velma had been washing and plaiting hair all morning long and hadn't gotten to Maxine yet. "I thought I would be left behind," Maxine recalled. But Carter wouldn't leave without her. She took Maxine to her own home, washed the eleven-year-old's hair, carefully combed it into braids, and got Maxine's clothes together. Maxine went to that picnic looking and feeling like somebody loved her. That gesture planted a seed: "And it stayed with me forever that she would do that.

"If you think that a teacher really cares about you, then you try to live up to their expectations," Maxine explained. "Ms. Carter had high expectations for me, and—especially after that picnic—I tried my best to live up to them."

One day, the class was given a writing assignment about health and nutrition—simple enough, right? The thing was that everyone else wrote their reports, which Miss Stokes advised should be "presentable to any person in the City of St. Louis," on crisp white paper tucked within store-bought binders. School supplies like that were considered "extravagant" in Maxine's home. Determined to do a good job regardless, Maxine got to work. She used construction paper given to her by Miss Stokes to fashion her own folder, which she decorated with images of fruit clipped from magazines. She then slid her report inside, punched holes along one side, and tied the entire thing together with a piece of leftover yarn given to her by a classmate who was knitting a scarf. When Maxine placed her homemade binder into Miss Stokes's hands, her teacher took a long look and smiled before turning to face the room.

"Look at this, class," Miss Stokes said. "Where there's a will, there's a way." According to Waters, everyone knew what she meant. Her pride was unmistakable, and it made Maxine feel "no less than ten feet tall."

From that height, Maxine kept excelling. She wanted to be two things when she grew up. The first was a dancer. Maxine took ballet and interpretive dance classes at her neighborhood community center. She loved Katherine Dunham, the dancer and anthropologist who pioneered African American modern dance. She also loved mezzo-soprano Grace Bumbry, so much so that she wrote an essay about the opera singer. Her high school English teacher was so impressed by the essay, she drove Maxine to the Bumbrys' home in St. Louis to show them. She was clearly attracted to elegance and power. Maxine's second career choice spoke to the latter: "I also wanted to be a social worker because, when we were on welfare, we were visited by social workers. It seemed like they had so much power." In the Carr-Moore home, visits from social workers were frequent. With a signature, the social workers dictated exactly how hard Maxine's family would have it that month. They loomed large.

They determined how much money Velma got and had the authority to come into her home and ask all sorts of personal questions. "They were perhaps the most important person you saw. They drove a car. Nobody in our neighborhood had a car. They wore nice clothes. They were educated. If they wanted to, they could make your life better or easier. So, why not want to be somebody who could do those things." What Maxine seemed to be in search of for most of her childhood was agency, control over her own destiny, her body, heck, her own wardrobe.

To that end, by age thirteen Maxine had started working in order to earn enough money to stop shopping at Goodwill with the rest of the Carr-Moore children. But let her tell it—Maxine Waters has "always" worked, honey. "You felt like you had to work because there was so little money, so little of everything," she recalled. "We were all eager to work when we were young. All of the kids in my neighborhood worked during the summer in various jobs. . . . We felt responsible for ourselves, and we weren't looking to our parents to go out and buy our clothes, or to buy a new bicycle for us, or new skates. We did it for ourselves. You know what I'm saying? We took a lot of responsibility at an early age for ourselves and our well-being," she said.

During the summer, some kids from the neighborhood picked strawberries in the fields outside the city. For her first real job, thirteen-year-old Maxine bused tables at Thompson's, a midwestern chain of segregated lunch counters, places where she wasn't legally allowed to eat. The cafeteria's slogan was "Eat Thompson's way for a better day!" On their lunch breaks, Maxine and the other black workers took their meals in the basement. "I just accepted it. That's the way it was," explained Waters, her thick skin showing.

But she wouldn't be busing tables for long. No one, least of all Maxine, saw that as her future. In 1956, the Vashon High School yearbook predicted that Maxine Carr would one day become Speaker of the House. In high school, Maxine had won a handful of oratory contests: Velma's major lesson—speak up for yourself—had paid off. Maxine even represented St. Louis in a regional competition. The girl could talk, and everyone knew it. "I think they saw Speaker," recalled Maxine, "as *speaker*." Either way, her entrée into politics would have to wait some two decades.

After graduating from Vashon High, one of two black high schools in St. Louis, Maxine met a GI named Edward Waters. Maxine was eighteen years old when she moved out of her mother's house to get married. The young couple's son, Edward, was born two years later, and three years after that came Karen. New opportunities, especially for black people, and St. Louis didn't mix at the time. "It was a dead end," Quincy Troupe, who graduated from Vashon a year after Maxine, told Helena in an interview. "Anybody who had any aspirations to be something beyond a worker left." In order to make the socioeconomic leap from working class to middle class, you had to leave St. Louis, Troupe explained. Some folks chose to stay close to home and headed to Chicago, some went to Detroit, and others made the trek all the way to New York. In 1961, Maxine and Edward, with their three-year-old son and infant daughter in tow, went west. It was a move similar to Velma's journey from small-town Arkansas some decades before.

Ed and Maxine settled in Southern California, specifically the predominantly African American neighborhoods south of downtown Los Angeles. Ed got a job in a printing plant, while Maxine clocked in at a garment factory. They were hardly living the dream, scrapping by on menial jobs with two small children to raise and no family around to help. After living in Los Angeles for a few years, Waters, now in her mid-twenties, would land a coveted gig as an operator at the Pacific Telephone Company, a job with career potential and a much bigger paycheck. Had a friend not told Maxine about a new federal program called Head Start, which provided low-income students with early childhood education, in Watts that was hiring, the future congresswoman might have enjoyed a fancy retirement party from Pacific Telephone some fifteen years ago. Instead, she decided to quit her cushy job at the phone company and, in 1966, become an assistant Head Start teacher at the sprawling Nickerson Gardens housing project on 114th Street in Watts, educating preschool children from low-income families much like the one she came from in St. Louis.

"Head Start changed my life," Waters said in an interview. "Through Head Start I discovered me." She was a firebrand from the beginning, organizing parents and community volunteers by teaching them how to advocate and fund-raise. The little girl who grew up in the close-knit community of Montrose Avenue, the one Velma had taught to speak up for herself and who found space for herself at the neighborhood rec center, and the teenager who won local oratory contests all came together at Head Start. There she wasn't just another cog in the machine, she was making a difference and doing it with people who looked like her, people she knew and loved even if they were strangers, because they reminded her so much of herself, of Velma. Working at the garment factory, Waters had been going through the motions of being a young wife and mother—passion wasn't playing a part in her day-to-day. That space she'd carved out for herself, and had come to love as a child, had grown tighter as the years went by. But now, with a risky move from corporate America to community organizing, Waters was finding that space again.

The world was changing and Maxine Waters was getting fired up. "It was exciting, exciting, exciting," she later said. "At that point in my life, I really began to examine where I was and what I really believed in." Community, for one, and making sure she was a part of it. In 1966 Waters enrolled at California State University in Los Angeles. The campus was all the way across town on the east side of the city. The trek to class would be long and frustrating for anyone— much less a mother of two with a full-time job and a whole husband at home. But she persisted.

Those years were predictably rough but also filled with possibility. Finally, Maxine was spinning the ambition she'd had since Montrose Avenue into something tangible and connected to the life she left behind in St. Louis. By the time Maxine got her bachelor's in sociology in 1971—a nod to those social workers she had feared and admired as a child—she and Ed had called it quits. "We were just on two different tracks after a while," she explained. The split was amicable, and the kids were all right. Now with a degree in hand and community organizing experience in the other, Maxine, thirty-three, went about putting her newfound purpose to good use, volunteering for Los Angeles city councilman Tom Bradley's bid to make history by becoming the city's first black mayor in 1973. He won that race with Maxine's help on the ground. Maxine then turned around and helped local businessman David Cunningham Jr. score the council seat Bradley had just left. And she was just getting started.

Life in Watts

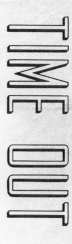

"1,000 RIOT IN L.A." On the morning of August 12, 1965, the front page of the *Los Angeles Times* bore the news in huge black letters that something in the city, indeed something in America, had broken. Violence, looting, and death would prevail in an impoverished South Central neighborhood for six days, the result of one ill-fated police stop and also decades of systemic oppression. Newspapers would capture images of a U.S. city reduced to rubble, like footage from a war zone, and reporters would try to explain to other citizens of the city and to the world at large how it all happened and what it meant. Practically speaking, it had started when two white police officers stopped a car near 116th Street and Avalon Boulevard, though the truth was that in some ways this uprising had been forming for years.

Marquette Frye, then twenty-one, and his brother Ronald had been driving home from a night on the town when Officer Lee Minikus pulled his car over for suspected drunk driving. Frye had been weaving, though he claimed he was trying to avoid potholes. By all accounts, the stop was both routine and almost friendly, even as the officer asked him to submit to a field sobriety test, which he did not pass, prompting an arrest. Frye's mother, Rena, arrived on the scene, having been informed by a neighbor about the stop. She scolded him for being drunk and suddenly his demeanor changed. Marquette began resisting the attempts to arrest him, backup arrived to assist Minikus, and soon they were fighting. People had gathered by this time and the crowd grew tense. Reports vary wildly about what happened in the next few moments. The physical altercation spread, pulling in Ronald and members of the crowd. Rena, coming to the defense of her son and stepson, jumped on at least one officer's back. The officers arrested all three Fryes; the rumor spread that an officer had shoved Rena. The crowd, then numbering in the hundreds, began to boo. As Marquette was being led away, he later recalled, one of his friends told him, "Don't worry; we're going to burn this mother down."

At this time in the 1960s, life in the predominantly black neighborhood of Watts was brutal. Jobs were scarce, poverty was rampant; the government had all but forgotten that the people who lived there even existed. "If I ever made enough money, I would move out of Watts like all the other big shots," a black middle-aged resident told a *Los Angeles Times* reporter months after the night the Fryes were arrested. "Los Angeles isn't all it's cracked up to be. Wherever you go, you're black—that's all there is to it." Another man, age twenty-seven, expressed similar frustration, saying, "I came from Mississippi. This ain't supposed to be Mississippi, but I run into damn near the same kind of treatment." The promise of California for many black residents, migrating from the South and the East, was proving to be a mirage, with the same racial discrimination, police brutality, and low wages, if any, that they thought they'd left behind. "Whites have everything," a twenty-year-old mother said. "If Negroes try to go into business, they're told they're not qualified. There's always something to keep Negro men down."

These sentiments, and more, were ever present in Watts, not even below the surface, stoking frustration, feelings of entrapment, and sometimes rage. And when Rena Frye leaped onto Lee Minikus's back on a sweltering August evening, that rage suddenly and fiercely had a target.

The crowd at Avalon and 116th began to throw rocks and pieces of concrete. The police, now numbering more than thirty, beat them back with batons. A police car at the corner of Imperial Boulevard and Avalon was set on fire. A revolt had begun.

The violence in Watts would last five more days, leaving the largely white-owned stores and businesses as burned-out shells. By the third day, the National Guard was called in to stanch the revolt, but in some ways had an exacerbating effect, killing some residents and isolating the area by blocking off streets like a war zone. Eventually, however, the might of the military overpowered the people, and the violence stopped.

LONG BEFORE SHE WOULD REPRESENT THE DISTRICT THAT INCLUDED Watts, Waters, then a new Los Angeles resident, bore witness to the unrest in the neighborhood that resulted in the deaths of thirty-four people. She'd seen how a police stop of a black man had escalated to a bloody altercation. She'd seen how distrust of the police force, misinformation, and outrage had stoked the nascent fire, causing the neighborhood to explode into days of violent uprising. She'd read the McCone Commission report, a 110-page investigation that set out to identify root causes, solutions, and ways to prevent such violence from ever happening again. Among the commission's recommendations: emergency literacy and preschool programs, improved police-community ties, increased low-income housing, and more job training projects, initiatives that would become the bedrock of her agenda as assemblywoman. Waters understood how interconnected issues of poverty, race, and justice are, and how long they can take to truly be reconciled.

By the time Waters first assumed elected office, the exterior of the South Central community where the uprising occurred in 1965 bore little to no trace of what had transpired. Buildings had been rebuilt; businesses

were, in some cases, reopened. The wreckage, at least externally, was cleared. But for the then assemblywoman, aesthetic changes weren't enough and wouldn't be enough to sustain Watts. There were still no prospects for many residents; there was still a critical lack of training; there was still a deficit of hope. Where were the jobs? If people couldn't work, couldn't put food on their tables, couldn't pay their electric bills, how were they supposed to make any progress? And absence of jobs often created a vacuum in a community into which the drug trade and gangs would gladly rush. And following that, violence: community members against community members and police officers against the people they are supposed to protect and serve.

Waters's approach to addressing these problems was multipronged and holistic. It was also, by necessity, painstaking. "To move families from generations of poverty takes even more than time," she would say decades later, looking back on the areas of progress and the areas that still ached for deliverance. "It takes times plus time."

In 1978, her first year in office, she accompanied President Jimmy Carter on a tour of a new Watts housing project. In his remarks, Carter highlighted some of the positive developments in labor and child care that his administration had brought to the area. He touted the statistic that the national unemployment rate had fallen 2 percentage points in the last year. But at the same time, the unemployment rate in Watts specifically was a staggering 60 percent. The America that some were experiencing was not reaching South Central Los Angeles.

Two years after his visit, Waters wrote to President Carter and asked him to create a "black ribbon" commission to study and address the epidemic of police violence against black people in America. Alongside statistics supporting her claims, she singled out the stories of Eulia Love, a Los Angeles resident who was shot by two members of the Los Angeles Police Department who came to her home to address a $22.09 utility bill, and Oakland resident Melvin Black, age fifteen, who was killed by a police officer who would, eight months later, shoot another Oakland resident in the back of the head. Carter did not win reelection the following year and the commission was never created.

NOVEMBER 1985 BROUGHT THE OPENING OF PROJECT BUILD, A MAJOR milestone for Waters and another attempt to address complex systemic issues in the 48th District. Project BUILD was a job training program Waters ran specifically for residents of the housing projects in her district. At the time, Nickerson Gardens, the largest of the city's housing projects, housed 1,500 unemployed people—nearly 40 percent of Nickerson Gardens's total population. Waters pointed out the mind-boggling fact that when the city wanted to make structural improvements and other rehabilitative changes to the projects, none of the workers it hired were from the area—she had to fight to get Nickerson residents included. "It's a struggle to say 'Look, you've got to have affirmative action. You've got to have jobs where these projects are going through,'" Waters said. But, she admonished, jobs were "very key to helping to solve the gang problem."

Not everyone saw things the way that Waters did, however. Police Chief Daryl Gates once held a press conference during which he addressed efforts to get job training for gang members, or as he referred to them, "little SOBs." "There are plenty of jobs out there," he said. Focus should be on "finding jobs for the good people." He did not clarify who the good people were, nor did he address the fact that the unemployment rate for black youths in Los Angeles in 1985 was over 41 percent.

Years later, Waters would recall the disconnect she sensed between the lived experiences of the people in the housing projects and the rhetoric about them. "There were several public housing projects and

supposedly we had programs at the city level that were dealing with job training and dealing with trying to get young people employed. But every time I went through, whether it was Nickerson Gardens, Contact Village, Imperial Courts, I could see nothing but young men hanging out. Hordes of young people. I kept thinking, why aren't the city resources getting here?"

Project BUILD sought to rectify the issue by directing state funds into a structure that would directly result in job acquisition. The program started out as a series of four-day seminars held at four housing projects—Jordan Downs, Nickerson Gardens, Imperial Courts, and Hacienda Village. Attendees were instructed by Waters herself on basic skills like filling out applications, interviewing, and managing the often unspoken dynamics of a professional environment. They were offered ten dollars per day to cover child care, and at the end of the seminars, Project BUILD would host graduation ceremonies, attended by potential employers and such luminaries as Jesse Jackson. The objectives were both practical and psychological. Participants were frequently reminded of their own worth and ability; Waters and the other instructors preached positivity, not as a facile Band-Aid, but as a lifeline. "We meet people who have been so beaten down by poor upbringing and bad surroundings, and have such a low-level tolerance for dealing with things like unemployment offices and filling out forms, that they don't even try," she said. "We know that these are fine people, but they are trapped people."

Drawing on knowledge affirmed during her years at Head Start, Waters also included remedial reading instruction in the Project BUILD curriculum, addressing the fact that, at the time, reading and math scores in South Central were among the lowest in the state. "The bureaucrats don't know what I'm talking about," she once remarked. "They think all you've got to do is connect these people with job training or school. The amazing thing we've learned at Project BUILD is that you have to first get these people to believe they have a shred of control over their environment or they won't take one step. That's why we hug them and tell them we care."

FOR WATERS, THE ISSUES FACING HER DISTRICT OUGHT TO HAVE inspired widespread moral outrage in the same way the apartheid struggle in South Africa did at the same time. "People don't want to talk about the injustice of what's going on in South-Central, because they really do believe we provide money for, say, education," she told the *Los Angeles Times.* "People believe that if there is a problem, it is their problem, it is not because we haven't done everything we can do for them." To her mind, what had been done was hardly enough—the employment options weren't enough, the attention to the relationship between police and the people of her community wasn't enough, and the education being made available wasn't enough. And she knew that she was uniquely positioned, as a powerful, connected leader, a black woman, and a persuasive politician, to try to move the needle, even just a little bit. "We have to learn how to play the game," she told a gathering of one thousand delegates at the African-American Summit in April 1989. "We have the power in many instances . . . if you dare to use it."

To wit, consider, if you will, this anecdote from a committee hearing in the late 1980s as further evidence of her passion, her commitment, and her laser-focused attention to the way structural oppression can affect every part of a person's life. Waters, in her position as chair of the Assembly Ways and Means Subcommittee, took to task the California Bicentennial Commission in the spring of 1987 after the commission promoted a textbook that included a 1934 essay that referred to black people as lazy and to black children as, shockingly, pickaninnies. The textbook was *The Making of America,* by W. Cleon Skousen, and the essay was by Fred Albert Shannon, who also, you may be interested to

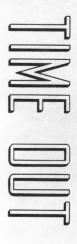

know, won the Pulitzer Prize for History in 1929 for writing about the Union army. So, perhaps the most generous reading of this material is that it showed the lack of nuance characteristic of the period in which it was produced. That period being both the 1930s, when the essay was written, and the 1980s, when the textbook was being printed and used for instruction. But who needs to be generous? Certainly not Assemblywoman Waters, who eliminated the commission's entire $50,000 budget in one fell swoop. "Do you think this 'pickaninny' is going to give you any money today?" she asked imperiously. Oh, for a time machine to hear these words delivered live.

Rejecting the commission members' protest, Waters continued: "Why should we trust you to educate the children about the foundation of this country?" And isn't that the crux of the issue here? Imagine Assemblywoman Waters speaking with the authority she held as the subcommittee's chair, and as a mother, and as a Head Start educator. This wasn't just about a word, a slur that the commission members insisted was being taken out of context. This was about trust. This was about a legislator's understanding of her role as guardian of the public's funds, the public's trust, and the public's future. When you look at the work of Maxine Waters's life, first in the California Assembly and later in Congress, the headlines often come from the attention-grabbing turns of phrase and sharp retorts, but the action behind the words is consistently driven by the pursuit of justice in the world.

During the first decade of her tenure in the Assembly, time and again she focused on ways that the lives of her constituents could be measurably improved through jobs, education, and advancement. Take, for example, the Maxine Waters Employment Preparation Center, which was founded as the Watts Skills Center and which she ran during her Assembly years. One building in Watts, however, did not solve the problems of the community she served. The problems were both granular and systemic. They were new every day and they were age-old. Waters knew that. "While I was [at the Employment Center] I learned an awful lot about how people were living and why they were living this way," she told Katie Couric in 2018. "First of all, real poverty, and second of all, lost hope. . . . They didn't think anybody cared about them."

Why should we trust you? This question is, perhaps, a lens through which one can view the legislation she pushed through during this period and the causes for which she advocated. Why should the people of her district trust their leaders to lead when social support programs failed them, when employment rates remained low and jobs scarce? When the education being planned for them was deeply flawed and showed obvious bias? When they could not even trust the police? "If you're black in America and not angry, you are crazy," Waters would later say at the African-American Summit. "We must not be afraid to be militant."

THE TIMELINE

1863

January 1: Three years into the American Civil War, President Abraham Lincoln issues the Emancipation Proclamation, declaring "all persons held as slaves within [any rebel state] shall be then, thenceforward, and forever free."

Emancipation Proclamation (del., lith. and print. by L. Lipman, Milwaukee, Wisconsin).

1865

The Thirteenth Amendment to the Constitution seals the deal and abolishes slavery and involuntary servitude, except as punishment for a crime.

1868

The Fourteenth Amendment grants all U.S. citizens, including the formerly enslaved, "equal protection of the laws."

1870

Senator Hiram Revels of Mississippi and Representative Joseph Rainey of South Carolina become the first

Senator Hiram R. Revels of Mississippi.

African Americans elected to Congress.

Mr. Revels showed no embarrassment whatever, and his demeanor was as dignified as could be expected under the circumstances. The abuse which had been poured upon him and on his race during the last two days might well have shaken the nerves of any one.
—*New York Times*

1896

May 18: The Supreme Court legalizes racial segregation by sanctioning what came to be known as the "separate but equal" doctrine in *Plessy v. Ferguson.*

1916

December 14: Velma Lee, Maxine's mother, is born in Cotton Plant, Arkansas, to Jack and Annie Mae Thomas.

1930s

Velma Lee marries Remus Carr Sr. The couple settles in St. Louis.

August 15, 1938: Maxine Carr is born, the fifth of her mother's thirteen children. Before Maxine's second birthday her father, Remus Sr., leaves the family.

My mother had a sixth-grade education, and she didn't always understand the needs of her children, necessarily. She often didn't understand me.

—Waters

1950

Apartheid, a system of institutional racism and oppression, becomes the law of the land in South Africa with the passing of the Population Registration Act, requiring all the country's citizens to be categorized by race.

1951

Maxine takes a job cleaning tables at Thompson's lunch counter in order to earn enough money to buy her own clothes. The thirteen-year-old is forced to eat her meals in the restaurant's basement.

1956

Maxine graduates from Vashon High School. The yearbook predicts that she will one day be Speaker of the House.

I think they saw Speaker as speaker.

—Waters

Maxine Carr marries GI Edward Waters.

1958

Edward Waters is born.

1961

Karen Waters is born.

Seeking new opportunities, the Waterses go west and settle in Southern California.

1965

As part of his War on Poverty, President Lyndon B. Johnson creates the Head Start program to aid underserved preschool children.

August 11: Racial tensions explode on a hot summer night after a white Highway Patrol officer arrests a black man in South Central Los Angeles. The ensuing six-day rebellion left thirty-four people dead and tens of millions of dollars in property damage.

1966

A friend tells Maxine about a new federal program called Head Start. Maxine quits her job as a telephone operator and becomes an assistant Head Start teacher in Watts.

Head Start changed my life. Through Head Start I discovered me.
—Waters

At that point in my life I really began to examine where I was and what I really believed in.
—Waters

Waters enrolls at California State University, Los Angeles. She majors in sociology because as a child growing up poor in Missouri, it was the social workers who had all the power.

1968

Shirley Chisholm of New York breaks the race and gender barrier and wins a seat in Congress. Six years later she runs for president of the United States.

Poster for presidential candidate Shirley Chisholm, 1972.

1972

Maxine divorces Ed Waters.

Barbara Jordan of Texas becomes the first African American woman elected to Congress from the Deep South.

All blacks are militant in their guts. But militancy is expressed in different ways.
—Barbara Jordan

Keynote address by Representative Barbara Jordan, Democratic National Convention, July 12, 1976.

1973

Maxine joins Tom Bradley's campaign to become the first black mayor of Los Angeles.

Maxine becomes Los Angeles councilman David Cunningham's chief deputy—her first official job in politics.

A MAN OF **QUALITY** is not threatened by a Woman for **EQUALITY**

Pin-back button for women's equality.

1976

Maxine is elected to the California State Assembly.

1977

Maxine marries Sidney Williams, a former linebacker for the Cleveland Browns who worked as an aide and chief of staff to Councilman Cunningham.

November: The young assemblywoman attends the first National Women's Conference in Houston, at which she helps lead the Black Women's Caucus.

1978

Maxine cofounds the Black Women's Forum, a nonprofit organization of more than 1,200 African American women in the Los Angeles area.

1984

Maxine becomes the first woman to chair the California Assembly's Democratic Caucus.

Jesse Jackson runs for president and Maxine serves as his national cochair and the chair of Jackson's California campaign.

Jesse Jackson, thank you for the leadership that you provided. It is because of you, and the hope that you created, that has caused Barack Obama to be the president today.
—Waters

1986

After a seven-year fight, Waters gets California to divest billions in pension funds connected to South African business interests, a colossal victory in the anti-apartheid divestment movement.

1990

November: With 79 percent of the vote, Maxine becomes the second African American woman to represent California's 29th District in the U.S. Congress and the sixth black woman elected to the House.

1991

Waters is appointed to the Financial Services Committee.

1992

April 29: The Los Angeles insurrection ignites in South Central Los Angeles after four LAPD officers are acquitted of assault, after being caught on camera brutally beating Rodney King.

May: Waters shows up uninvited to a White House meeting about "urban issues" in the wake of the Los Angeles uprising.

I don't intend to be excluded or dismissed.
—Waters

Placard from March on Washington, August 28, 1963.

At a panel discussion about black civic engagement, Waters calls President George H. W. Bush a "racist."

July 15: Maxine seconds the nomination of Democratic presidential candidate Bill Clinton.

1994

Sidney Williams is appointed as the U.S. ambassador to the Bahamas under President Clinton.

July 30: After a heated exchange with Republican congressman Peter King on the House floor about the treatment of women in Congress, Waters is threatened with "the presentation of the Mace."

We are now in this House. We are members of this House. We will not allow men to intimidate us and to keep us from participating.
—Waters

August: Waters votes against President Clinton's infamous federal crime bill.

1997

Maxine becomes chair of the Congressional Black Caucus.

1998

Waters helps create the Minority AIDS Initiative, establishing $156 million in funds to combat the spread of the disease in minority communities.

2002

October 10: Maxine votes against the Iraq War.

We are going to be criticized, and there will be those who even call us unpatriotic.
—Waters

2008

Waters introduces the Stop Very Unscrupulous Loan Transfers from Underprivileged countries to Rich, Exploitive Funds (Stop VULTURE) Act.

2009

The House Ethics Committee opens an investigation into whether Maxine sought bailout funds for a bank that her husband, Sidney Williams, held stock in.

2011

At a community event in her district, Waters says, "The Tea Party can go straight to hell."

2012

Waters is cleared in the House Ethics Committee investigation.

2014

With bipartisan support between coastal Democrats and Republicans, Waters gets the Homeowner Flood Insurance Affordability Act passed.

2017

January: After a classified hearing, Waters declares during a thirty-second press conference that FBI director James Comey "has no credibility," then she exits stage left.

February: Waters becomes one of the first members of Congress to call for President Trump's impeachment.

He's a liar! He's a cheat! He's a con man. We've got to stop his ass!
— Waters

March 28: Fox News host Bill O'Reilly insults Waters by calling her hair a "James Brown wig." Waters responds to O'Reilly, "I'm a strong black woman and I cannot be intimidated."

April 19: O'Reilly is fired amid sexual harassment allegations.

July 27: While questioning Treasury secretary Steve Mnuchin during a House Financial Services Committee hearing, Waters utters her most famous three words to date— "Reclaiming my time."

2019

Three decades after joining, Waters becomes chair of the House Financial Services Committee.

I have the gavel.
— Waters

November 13: The House conducts its first public hearing in the formal impeachment inquiry against President Donald J. Trump.

December 18: The House votes to impeach President Donald J. Trump.

CHAPTER THREE

MS. WATERS GOES TO SACRAMENTO

1965–1976

IN WHICH THE COMMUNITY ORGANIZER FIGHTS
THE ESTABLISHMENT AND EMERGES A POWERFUL
AND ADMIRED ASSEMBLYWOMAN WHO WILL MAKE
YOU QUAKE IN YOUR BOOTS

After joining Head Start in 1966, serving as an assistant teacher and later a supervisor at the center located in the soon-to-be-infamous Nickerson Gardens housing project, Waters caught the bug. It had been just a year since the deadly Watts Revolt (also known as the Watt Riots to the *un*woke). The streets were still smoldering from the rebellion that erupted when a highway patrolman's arrest of a young black motorist turned violent, exposing deep racial and economic tensions in the community that detonated into six days of local unrest.

Tasked with organizing parents in the community in the wake of the revolt, the girl from St. Louis settled into her place as a South L.A. activist, fund-raising for the grassroots nonprofits the Mothers of Watts and the Black Congress, which had sprung up amid the chaos. Head Start, she said, "brought me in touch with the politicians, and I learned about which politicians were great and were supportive, and which ones were not. That took me into volunteering in campaigns for those politicians that I thought were supportive." Maxine, who grew up in and out of the projects and knew poverty's face well enough, was uniquely qualified to bridge the gap between community activism and campaigning.

In 1966, buildings were still caving in on themselves when Waters attended a meeting more than a hundred miles away in Bakersfield, organized by the charismatic Northern California assemblyman Willie Brown. That meeting gathered together a who's who of black political movers and shakers (Representative Augustus F. Hawkins, future Los Angeles mayor Tom Bradley), plus folks whom "the movement" had identified as the new generation of political power. Their main strategy? Unify the electorate, consolidate power muscle, and work inside the system for systematic change. Waters had been tapped.

"There's only one way for the cause of Negroes to be advanced in the Democratic Party: Rock the boat!" Brown exhorted at that meeting. "What we do here," he continued, "could very well demonstrate how much power we have in the Democratic Party." Waters recalled wanting to challenge Brown, who claimed in that same speech that the Southern California black activists weren't being aggressive enough politically, but she held her tongue—for a while. Eventually the pair would become practically inseparable allies in the California State Assembly, but that was a decade away. In the meantime, the Head Start teacher from Watts was called to action. As a community facilitator for the program, Waters attended "encounter groups," organized get-togethers popularized in the 1960s that focused on individual participants tapping in to their personal feelings. (Note to millennials: the concept was revolutionary at the time.) Those meetings served a singular purpose for Waters, who was on the verge of discovering who she really wanted to be. "I really started to state what I thought," Maxine recalled in Eleanor Clift and Tom Brazaitis's *War Without Bloodshed.*

"I remember at some point deciding that I had been silenced by this need to be liked and not wanting to step on anyone's toes or hurt anybody's feelings. What I discovered is I really don't care whether people like me or not. It freed me up," she added. Unburdened and unbothered by the expectations of her race, class, or gender, Waters, in essence, started doing her. She became a fixture on the local campaign scene—walking the precincts, knocking on doors, and passing out pamphlets for candidates she believed would help the cause. Waters quickly made a name for herself as someone with incredibly strong ties to South L.A.'s African American community.

"She knew everybody," Raphael Sonenshein, who worked with Maxine in the mid-1970s, recalled in an interview with Helena. "And not in the way politicians know everybody. She *knew* people, people she had helped when she was in the Head Start program. And they all called her Maxine." After managing the back-to-back winning campaigns of Mayor Tom Bradley's allies, former journalist Robert Farrell and businessman David Cunningham Jr., Waters followed the trail downtown to city hall. A longtime friend of Bradley's, Cunningham, whose biggest rival was *Star Trek* actor George Takei, was a relative political unknown before winning the new mayor's old city council seat. Bradley, who wanted allies on the council, strategically placed Waters in a key role in the local businessman's campaign to help shore up his African American voting base, and she delivered.

In 1973, Cunningham appointed Waters his chief deputy, and in no time flat Waters became one of the highest-ranking black women downtown. In Cunningham's office, Waters was known as the woman with the answers. "The thing about Maxine Waters," Rick Taylor, who worked with her in Cunningham's office and on Bradley-backed local campaigns, told Helena in an interview, "from the day I met her when she was just starting to today, she was always smarter than the rest of us." Waters was heralded as a decision maker who could think ten miles ahead of everyone else. Often when asked to come up with a quick solution on the spot, Taylor had a stock answer at the ready: "I'm not Maxine Waters, I've got to think about it."

In city hall, Maxine's own political muscle was reaching P90X levels. Meetings started when she got there. If you pissed her off, you got a call from her desk and never made that mistake again. Getting Maxine's endorsement for any city or county-wide office became a prerequisite if you wanted the support of South Los Angeles. "When Maxine spoke, everybody listened and everybody took another look at what they were about to do," Zev Yaroslavsky, a former L.A. councilman whose office was on the same floor as Cunningham's, recalled in an interview with Helena. "Anybody who underestimated her would live to regret it, but over time I don't think that was ever an issue."

o it was, a decade after she joined Head Start and just three years since entering city hall, that Maxine Waters ran for public office. And she did it in the most Maxine Waters way possible—by calling bullshit. It was February 1976 and Leon Ralph, the powerful five-term assemblyman from L.A.'s 48th, was having a crisis of conscience. Ralph, forty-three, had served nearly a decade in Sacramento and wasn't sure if he could go on doing it. The ministry had been calling the assemblyman since he was a young man and Ralph wanted to answer. "I couldn't keep doing both," he told the *Los Angeles Times*. "I'd be shortchanging either the Lord or my constituents." A Sophie's choice, if you will. But here's the thing: the would-be preacher hadn't bothered to disclose this raging internal battle with anyone publicly, much less the candidates waiting in the wings. Ralph was incredibly popular in the 48th and powerful in Sacramento, serving as chairman of the Assembly Rules Committee. No Democrat would even think to run against him. The only way Ralph's seat would ever be on the chessboard was if he gave it up voluntarily. He knew all that on that February day, which also just so happened to be the deadline to file for candidacy. So, essentially, the veteran politician ran out the clock as he contemplated whether to run again.

With less than thirty minutes left before the deadline, Ralph and his trusted legislative aide, twenty-five-year-old Johnny Collins, walked across the street to the secretary of state's office to file his candidate intention form and submit $232.32 for the filing fee. In his telling, Ralph got to the office and had a come-to-Jesus moment— literally. The clock was ticking on the 5 P.M. deadline.

"When I arrived at the desk to pay it, I just could not. I could not go forward with seeking a sixth term as an assemblyman. I turned to Johnny and I said, 'Johnny, I can't do it. I just can't. I know that I need to go and answer the call for the ministry. Here's a check. It was made out for me. Why don't you take it and run?'" Right. Ralph announced his retirement after the 5 P.M. deadline while also handing the baton to his heir apparent—without anyone the wiser. No one else, Democrat or Republican, had filed to oppose Ralph, because no one knew the man was leaving office.

Sonenshein was with Waters at the office at city hall when she got wind of this foolishness. Suffice it to say she was not happy. As she saw it, Ralph's out-of-the-blue retirement and Collins's electric slide on to the ballot was "boss politics," shady backdoor deals to keep power concentrated in one camp. Not to mention that the political anointing had landed on a twenty-five-year-old kid. Nope. "Everyone knew she was thinking of running," said Sonenshein. The temperature in the office shot up to Bikram Yoga level. "Then we discovered that Maxine had a lot of friends," added Sonenshein. Not missing a beat, Waters picked up the phone and dialed the secretary of state, March Fong Eu. "Something's wrong with this picture," she told Eu, who had become the first woman and first Asian American elected California's secretary of state two years earlier. Eu was the woman in charge of the state's elections, tasked with keeping the process transparent and fair. Unsurprisingly, she wasn't having it, either. At Waters's and other enraged would-be candidates' behest, Eu extended the filing deadline for another five days, giving everyone else a chance to officially throw their hat in the ring.

"That was their first mistake," said Sonenshein of Collins's campaign. "Our side was riled up and it hadn't worked." Waters and her tight-knit team would make the filing deadline okey-doke a major sticking point on the campaign trail. This was "machine politics" at its most machine-y, a veteran politician trying to hand over the keys to the district. No, ma'am.

After the initial bait-and-switch, maybe the second most infuriating aspect of the campaign was that the powers that be labeled

Waters an underdog, which was crazy to her supporters and staff. "If Collins is the front runner," Narda Zacchino wrote in the *Los Angeles Times,* "Maxine Waters is breathing down his neck." There were other Democrats and one Republican in the race, but this fight was between Maxine and Johnny—or by proxy, the separate black political factions angling for power in Los Angeles and in California at large. On one side there was Lieutenant Governor Mervyn Dymally, who'd built a powerful statewide African American political organization with the help of working-class blacks in Los Angeles. On the other was Los Angeles mayor Tom Bradley, who was consolidating local power in the state's largest city with the help of middle-class African Americans and white supporters from the wealthy West Side. Collins was a Dymally candidate. Maxine, even without his official endorsement, was Bradley's. So, in 1976, the 48th Assembly District race was about more than just this one race. It was about which black political machine would come out on top.

But still? Collins? The front-runner? Here was a twenty-five-year-old aide whose résumé was sparse, including a summer internship, *internship,* at the State House, running against a thirty-eight-year-old who'd risen to become one of the most powerful staffers in city hall. It was outrageous, but not at all unexpected. "The assumption," recalled Sonenshein, "was it's not your time, it's not the right time, maybe next time. Of course, they had no idea."

From jump the Waters campaign was a nimble beast. She was "a happy warrior," said Sonenshein, "a force of nature." She walked the precincts, shook hands, and listened, like, really listened. "Maxine! Maxine!" was a common refrain from the trail. Voters called out to her with the kind of warm familiarity usually reserved for an old friend, not a photo-opping politician. Oftentimes the candidate would look over and know the name of the person calling her from the clipped front lawn or stucco storefront. This is where Waters's community organizer roots began to really show. She came to the role of candidate from the bottom up; her framework was one of inclusion and insurgency. Her job was to represent and fight from the inside. She talked how her constituents talked. "She was a person who was a person before they were a politician," Sonenshein explained. She took on their causes big or small, showing up to community meetings when no other candidate would, listening to folks complain about a behemoth redevelopment that was pushing them out or a liquor store nobody wanted in the neighborhood. "She has a very sensitive nose on how to be on the right side of her constituency," explained Yaroslavsky, the veteran L.A. politician who's known Waters for decades. "I don't know anybody who is more in sync with her constituency."

Collins, who grew up in Watts and attended Jordan High School on East 103rd, tried to paint Maxine as a carpetbagger, an outsider. Campaign materials from the Collins camp urged voters "not be fooled by latecomers who have just moved into the district." It was a burn. Waters had moved from tony Baldwin Hills, a black middle-class enclave, back to Watts in order to run. "I did move back," Waters told the *Los Angeles Times*. "It's nothing I try to hide. I moved back in because I felt Leon Ralph and Lt. Gov. Mervyn Dymally had gone a little too far by trying to take that district and give it to someone without the voters participating in that decision." That's a really nice way to say "yeah *and*."

"My roots are here," continued Waters, trotting out her Watts bona fides. She'd worked in Nickerson Gardens. People knew her. She talked like them. Mayor Bradley, on whose campaign Waters had cut her teeth, did not formally endorse Maxine's bid for Sacramento. Most likely Bradley was still reeling from the nail-biting loss that another local candidate he supported suffered the year before. But his official thumbs-up proved to be unnecessary. Maxine got his wife, Ethel Bradley, on board, and the rest of the mayor's support network was behind her. The city's preeminent African American newspapers, the *Los Angeles Sentinel* and the *Wave*, officially backed her as well.

Waters started her campaign with a $10,000 loan from Cunningham, her old boss, and steadily fund-raised for the next six months until the primary in June. But still, no one had tons of money in those days. This was a five-figure race, not a radio and TV ad operation. Instead, Waters sent out seeds. Yes, literal seeds. Waters and seeds.

Overwhelmingly Democratic and mostly impoverished, the 48th District spanned South Los Angeles, including Watts and the suburbs of Lynwood and Southgate (read: where white people lived). Though mostly African American, the district had a smattering of white and Latino voters as well.

"We had to figure out how to run without a lot of money. It was a time of gardens. Everybody was getting interested in raising their food and being more nutrition conscious," Waters recalled in an interview with Shonda Rhimes. The campaign ordered twenty-five-pound sacks and mailed a handful of seeds out in little envelopes to voters across the district. White folks got carrot seeds, the Latinos got cilantro, and black people got collard greens. "We mailed them and at that time the postman would laugh because they were carrying the mail around and these seeds were shaking in their mailbags," she said. For years afterward constituents would come up to Waters, who still walks the precincts, and tout the collard green stalks growing in their backyards. "Because collard green stalks last for a long time, and they keep growing, and they keep producing," she explained.

In South Gate, a white conservative enclave, Maxine's camp sent volunteers, many of them white women, to knock on doors. One such campaign worker, Waters recalled, asked the white man who answered the door if he would vote for Maxine Waters, who was a relative unknown in that part of town. They had this exchange:

"Is she a . . . [n-word]?" asked the voter.

"No," said the volunteer, "she's a woman."

"OK!" Done and done.

Back at campaign HQ the staff laughed about the story. In the end, Waters would win South Gate handily, with 60 percent of the two-party vote that November.

Still, Maxine knew where her bread was buttered. Black women remained her target audience always. "We had our whites in the white community, they were significant voters, but the black women in the district, I listened very carefully to them, and I started to put their wording back into campaign literature. They would see me, I would talk to them, and they would say, 'Why not a woman?' I'd do my literature: Why not? Why not a woman? Connecting back with them," she recalled.

Maxine considered herself a feminist, which for a black woman in the 1970s was as radical as an Afro. "For me to identify myself as a feminist back in the day, black women said, 'What are you talking about. You can't be a feminist. That's a white woman's thing,'" she said in an interview with Gloria Steinem. Maxine saw the irony there. It was women who'd encouraged her to run for office in the first place, as the feminist movement was gaining traction. "I mean, all of those women just let me in," she reminisced in an interview with Shonda Rhimes, "and I just followed them and worked with them and they became some of my biggest supporters, you know? . . . And the black women were not considered feminists, but they really were." Black women whose names still sit with Waters today include Watts activist Mary B. Henry, who helped President Johnson first create the Head Start program; Opal Jones, the antipoverty activist and social worker; and community leader Lillian Harkless Mobley, who spearheaded the group of women that pushed to create the Martin Luther King Jr./Drew Medical Center. "I met wonderful women," said Waters, recalling her work in Watts. "I live with them all the time even though they're all dead. I mean I know them so well, I think about them."

To the surprise of no one, including Johnny Collins's campaign, on June 8, 1976, Maxine Waters won the Democratic primary, cinching her seat in the State Assembly. She earned 48.2 percent of the vote to Collins's 37.3 percent. The final score tallied 14,641 for Waters and 11,322 for Collins. She beat the brakes off him in what the *Los Angeles Times* called "perhaps the biggest upset of the day." With Maxine's victory, the number of women in the California State Assembly would grow from three to nineteen.

"It's really a simple matter of Collins not having experience," she told the *Los Angeles Times*. "They tried to make him something he wasn't. He's a nice young man. But he didn't know the community and I'm an old campaign manager and I knew who gives the money and how to raise money and Collins just couldn't match me." Bloop. She hasn't had a serious challenger since.

On her very first day in Sacramento, Maxine Waters stood up to introduce a piece of legislation that would officially change the title of the mostly men, and some women, of the chamber to "assembly member," as opposed to the antiquated and obviously sexist "assemblyman." The room was so shocked they voted for it, 48 to 27. Eventually, though, the fog lifted, and the men got their collective suits in a bunch. "Men attacked me viciously," Waters told Diane Seo. "They charged me with trying to neuter the male race." After reopening debate, the motion was overturned, 41 to 26. Fine, whatever. Waters had still gotten her point across. She hadn't come to play.

The National Women's Conference of 1977

Dressed in a slim-cut black suit with a deep purple butterfly collar brushing her shoulders, thirty-nine-year-old Maxine Waters sliced through the roaring crowd of the arena floor and stepped up to the mic like a battle rapper. "Madame Chairperson, I am Assemblywoman Maxine Waters, delegate from the state of California," she announced in a clear voice that snapped to attention the thousands upon thousands gathered at Houston's Sam Houston Coliseum. Oh, it's about to go down.

Held over four days in November 1977, the National Women's Conference was a federally funded meeting of the feminist minds meant to define the whole of the women's rights agenda. "It was a constitutional convention for the female half of the country," Gloria Steinem, one of the event's organizing commissioners, recalled in her memoir. The goal was to create a slate of gender parity recommendations that would then land on the desk of President Jimmy Carter. So, like, no big deal or whatever. The last time women from across the country had gathered like this was in Seneca Falls, New York, at the very first women's rights convention—in 1848 under the leadership of suffragist Elizabeth Cady Stanton.

Nearly 130 years later, Waters found herself not only among the lionesses of the movement—Congresswoman Bella Abzug, author Betty Friedan, poet Maya Angelou, and civil rights icon Coretta Scott King— but at center stage. Maxine had been in the California legislature for less than a year before she had been selected as one of the two thousand female delegates chosen the previous summer at satellite conferences in fifty states and six territories to head to Houston with a laundry list of recommendations. In 1977, under the watchful eyes of fifteen thousand observers, the delegates, who represented one of the most diverse cross sections of American women to ever gather in one place, passionately debated and passed resolutions on a National Plan of Action consisting of twenty-six "planks," or policy totem poles, that covered everything from the Equal Rights Amendment to affordable child care to access to credit.

Plank No. 17, the Minority Plank, needed some work.

Before the Houston conference, the women of color delegates who fell under the minority umbrella—Native American, Alaskan native, Hispanic, black, Asian American, and Pacific Islander women—had never come together to create a unified agenda specifically addressing their needs. Too often they were "the invisible women" behind the scenes of the movement, very rarely stepping out front to voice their own concerns and desires. Since the Minority Plank represented them all, they would need to articulate and condense their common and disparate issues, from racism and poverty to language discrimination and tribal autonomy. It was a heavy lift. Somehow Steinem, forty-three, was conscripted into service. Serving as a scribe, the veteran journalist bounced from hotel room to hotel room "writing down concerns that were shared by all, combining language for their approval and appending issues that were unique to each." To come up with this all-encompassing Minority Plank, the women-of-color caucuses had to meet late at night after the official business of the conference was over in order to not miss key floor votes on the other important planks in the national plan. It was a boatload of extra work jammed into an already packed four-day schedule. Maxine Waters stood out as a major player, coalescing the massive three-hundred-member black caucus.

Minutes before the new and improved Minority Plank was to be presented in the arena, floor representatives from each caucus met to okay the final language. Waters kicked things off. According to the conference's official report, the young assemblywoman's "clear, strong voice" could be heard from the back of the hall demanding recognition. "The noisy floor grew quiet as she began to read the umbrella statement

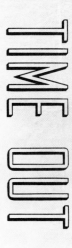

applying to all minorities, an honor for which she had been chosen in recognition of the no-sleep energy she had put into helping the women come together in Houston," read *The Spirit of Houston*, the official report of the convention that was sent to President Carter.

"The united minority caucus of International Women's Year Conference 1977 move to substitute the resolution on minority women as it is presented in the proposed plan of action and we would like to substitute that as follows . . ." began Waters, who then schooled the arena filled with nearly twenty thousand women, men, and children on intersectionality.

"Minority women share with all women the experience of sexism as a barrier to their full rights of citizenship. . . . But institutionalized bias based on race, language, culture and/or ethnic origin or governance of territories or localities has led to the additional oppression and exclusion of minority women and to the conditions of poverty from which they disproportionately suffer. Therefore every level of government action should recognize and remedy this double discrimination and ensure the right of each individual to self-determination," Waters said slowly and clearly as she read from the preamble of the Minority Plank hundreds of women had spent the last two nights composing. It was a word. Church had begun.

Quickly the gathered news media there caught on to the fact that something special was happening, and they rushed to fill in the aisle in front of the microphone these women had transformed into a pulpit. For the first time minority women were standing in solidarity while also speaking their own individual truths within the larger context of the feminist movement. After Waters came representatives from the other women-of-color caucuses reading their own contributions to the subject, name-dropping the Earth Mother, sweat shop conditions, underpaid farm-working women, and mothers deported from their U.S.-born children.

The last woman to speak emerged from the crowd with a bodyguard in tow. Coretta Scott King, Martin Luther King Jr.'s widow, looked every bit the icon when she arrived at the microphone reading from the resolution "on behalf of the black women of America." King spoke about affirmative action, education, and unemployment. After asking the chair to adopt the minority women's substitute resolution, King added, "Let this message go forth from Houston and spread all over this land. There is a new force, a new understanding, a new sisterhood against all injustice that has been born here." The resolution was nearly unanimously adopted. The floor exploded in applause. Folks were sobbing. Delegates rose to their feet, reaching for the hands of women across the wide aisles to jointly raise them in the air in triumph. Someone started the first lines of the civil rights anthem "We Shall Overcome." Do you have the chills yet?

That moment was the highest of the four-day conference and Maxine Waters was right in the middle of it.

"ANYBODY WHO UNDERESTIMATED HER WOULD LIVE TO REGRET IT..."

CHAPTER FOUR

INTERNATIONAL IMPLICATIONS

1979–1986

IN WHICH OUR FAVORITE AMERICAN LEADER USES HER PLATFORM TO EFFECT CHANGE IN SOUTH AFRICA, OFTEN AGAINST THE POLITICAL TIDE right and early on January 3, 1985, Maxine Waters rolled up on the South African consulate in Beverly Hills with six other community leaders. They rode the elevator up to the sixth floor of the tall white building on Wilshire Boulevard and then, outside the office of the consulate, they unpacked some water, tuned a little radio, pushed some sleeping bags against the wall, popped open folding chairs, and sat down. This wasn't a coffee klatch or a cookout; they weren't there to shoot the breeze. This was a sit-in. Or perhaps it was a camp-in, considering the sleeping bags. Either way, the group of activists wasn't there for leisure, there was no merit badge to be earned, and no one would be telling ghost stories around a fire. The reality of life for millions of black South Africans had been a real-life horror story for far too long, and this group had arrived as part of an escalating series of protests to declare that enough was enough.

By this time in her career as a politician and activist, Waters had firmly established herself as a force to be reckoned with. As a testament to her persuasiveness, she'd become majority whip of the California Assembly, making her fourth ranked on the leadership team; additionally, she chaired a number of important committees, including Ways and Means. As an assemblywoman, from the earliest moments of her tenure Maxine Waters had prioritized liberation for her people in all forms.

Soon after taking office in 1976, she had set her sights on eliminating police brutality—a campaign that would continue throughout her career—and she championed education as a ladder out of poverty. Waters understood that she, as a leader in general and as a black woman in particular, was in a unique position to draw attention to structural injustice and to effect change. She was tireless in this respect. When in Sacramento, she'd start her days at 8 A.M.

and wouldn't leave until twelve hours later, sometimes more—even when the Assembly wasn't in session. She walked through her precincts every Saturday, speaking to her people. She advocated, hard, for their needs. Waters understood the bold strategies of community organizing and the negotiation and compromise needed to achieve success in state-level diplomacy. But she also knew that authentic and effective advocacy for black people was anathema to politics as usual. She knew how to play the game, but she also knew she'd have to flip the board over.

Further, Waters understood that her people weren't just those who lived within her district—just as systemic oppression doesn't observe the lines on maps. South Africa was always on her mind, as were the 24 million black South Africans living under apartheid in 1985. About this, as with so many other justice issues, Waters was impatient for change. The white supremacist authoritarian government that segregated and persecuted black South Africans had been in power since 1948. Under apartheid, South African law broke the population up into four racial categories: black South Africans, whites, coloreds (meaning largely people of mixed racial heritage), and Asians. The laws dramatically disenfranchised nonwhites, forcing them off the land they occupied and into slums, stripping them of the right to vote, and requiring that they carry passes to travel. Though by the early 1980s, 72 percent of the nation's population was made up of black South Africans, the minority apartheid government kept them socially, economically, and politically oppressed, having stolen their land and resettled them in shantytowns, and smothering peaceful protests with arrests and violent police action.

Waters saw the liberation of the "most oppressed, racist nation in the world" as an immediate moral priority. It could not wait a minute more. In 1979, shortly after being elected, she put her power where her heart was by introducing a bill that would require the state to divest from any companies that did business in South Africa. She could not get a single vote in the Assembly. Yet she was undeterred; she would keep reintroducing the bill, or similar legislation, for years; she would support the work of American student activists and South African opposition leaders like Bishop Desmond Tutu; she would speak, and rally, and slowly but surely secure the votes of her colleagues. And, in cases where that didn't work, she would sit outside the consulate and refuse to leave until she was heard.

That January morning in 1985 was not Waters's first time at the South African consulate; protests of this sort had been going on with increased frequency for much of the fall and winter of 1984 at consulates in California, Washington, D.C., and Seattle, among others, and Waters had participated before. The escalation was part of a concerted strategy by organizations like the Los Angeles Free South Africa Movement, which Waters would soon chair, to lift the issue of South African liberation to the level of national conversation in the United States after years of mounting outrage. Progress was incremental, but it was progress nonetheless. The actions Waters and others took were garnering more press coverage; protests on college campuses like the University of California, Berkeley, were growing in frequency and intensity. It was no longer a question of whether the United States would take action on apartheid; it was becoming a question of when.

At the consulate, Waters was joined by Bishop H. H. Brookings of the African Methodist Episcopal Church; Danny J. Bakewell of the Los Angeles Brotherhood Crusade; Mary B. Henry from the Compton school board; David Mixner, a public relations expert; Abenaa Poindexter of the Black Women's Forum, an education task force founded by Waters; and Bernard Walker, president of the Black

Student Union at the University of Southern California. Their demand was simple: they wanted to speak with South African consul general Les Labuschagne in the presence of reporters. Waters had spoken with Labuschagne privately earlier in the week, but he had resisted a public meeting. So they camped, and they waited, and they periodically descended to the lobby to make statements to the gathered press. Speaking from within the consulate's elevator so as not to risk getting locked out if she emerged, she made a promise there was no doubt she would deliver on: "You will see a continued escalation."

"BUT ABOVE ALL, ECONOMIC PRESSURE"

Later that spring, Bishop Desmond Tutu stood in front of the California Assembly, his voice echoing off the chamber walls, racked with pain, infused with passion, begging. "Please," he cried out, "please, please, for goodness' sake, help us." The religious leader and activist from Johannesburg, who the year prior had been awarded the Nobel Peace Prize, was in America for the college graduation of his daughter in Kentucky. He'd taken the opportunity of a transatlantic visit to rally the cause he worked for tirelessly at home. He spoke in front of eight thousand students at UC Berkeley, delivered statements to the press, and implored the powerful to act decisively on what he called an Armageddon in South Africa. He warned that if violence broke out in the increasingly fraught political climate of his home country, it would spill over into America. Indeed, by this point protests on college campuses, which had begun as early as 1973, were proving unmanageable to campus police and, on campuses like Berkeley, Columbia, and Rutgers, had become violent. At issue in the university protests were the endowments, which contained billions of dollars in investments in South African companies and companies that did business in the country. Profiting off the oppressive government was, for many, a moral outrage. Tutu told the students in quads the same thing he told the joint session of the California Assembly: freeing South Africa would take pressure—political pressure, diplomatic pressure, but above all, economic pressure.

The amount of money that the State of California had already invested in South Africa, between employee pensions and the university system, was staggering. UC Berkeley alone had $1.7 billion in investments in South Africa; California public employees had $5.2 billion in companies that did business with South Africa; the state's teachers had $2.6 billion. Divestiture would be more than a powerful statement; it would have a direct fiduciary impact. Opponents argued that any negative effect of divestiture would be felt less by the government of South Africa and more by the workers, particularly black workers. They also pointed out that the cost would blow back on the American institutions trying to do the right thing—Berkeley stood to lose $100 million if it sold all of its South Africa–associated investments. But advocates, like Waters, saw it as a necessary escalation for an issue that had resisted diplomatic resolution for decades. Moreover, as Tutu said, South Africa's woes would not respect the borders of South Africa. "The dollars of any American firm invested in South Africa are at great risk," Waters pointed out. "There is a tremendous potential for loss." This was also America's problem.

As chairwoman of Ways and Means and a member of the Assembly Committee on Public Investments, Finance, and Bonded Indebtedness, Maxine Waters was uniquely positioned to act on Tutu's last and most consequential request. Once again, she introduced her bill that would prevent the new investment of state pension funds in companies doing business privately in South Africa or with the government of South Africa unless said companies cut all ties to the nation. She also authored a bill that would require sale of any previously held investments in the country by January 1, 1987. Unlike her first attempt, six years earlier, this time Waters's efforts were gaining traction. As spring approached in 1985, it looked like the bill might actually pass. At the same time, she took strategic aim at the University of California system and its investments in South Africa. "It is so important," she told a group of three thousand outside Berkeley's Sproul Hall that April, "for you to know that you are not alone in the struggle." Though the UC Board of Regents controlled the finances and investments outside of the purview of government oversight, as an assem-

Waters in her office in the California State Assembly in 1987.

blywoman, Waters had the power to attach provisos onto any new funding that the state sent the university system's way. Did she use that power? Absolutely. Before a transfer of $85 million went to the UC system that year, Waters made sure to include the stipulation that none of it could be invested in any South Africa–affiliated companies.

While by the mid-1980s students throughout the country had made their position on apartheid clear, inside the halls of power, taking financial steps to pressure South Africa's government was still seen as a Far Left initiative, and many on both sides of the aisle were hesitant to pledge support for Waters's bill, even as the Committee on Public Investments, Finance, and Bonded Indebtedness voted in favor of it and it moved on to Ways and Means. Did this stop her? Absolutely not. So fired up was she over this issue that she made sure that a proposal got into the state budget requiring California to sell off any of the state pension systems' investments in companies doing business with South Africa. She was going to make this happen, one way or another.

Some of her fellow Democrats weren't so sure that the budget was the right place to make this effort. A two-house legislative conference committee was convened to hammer out issues with the budget, which included a request for a $1 billion reserve by the Republican governor George Deukmejian and Waters's South Africa proviso. The committee chair, State Senator Alfred Alquist, a Democrat, was sour on the idea of any reference to South Africa making it into the state's budget. "My personal opinion is we can't solve all of the problems of the world here in this California Legislature," he argued. For days, the committee debated the issue until Alquist, at the encouragement of Waters and Assemblyman John Vasconcellos, switched his position, but on the condition of a compromise. The state would not be required to sell off South African investments right away: state pension fund administrators would have until January 1 to end all new investments in South Africa and until July 1 of the following year to adopt a plan for divestment in companies that provided military supplies used for oppressive purposes or to support the apparatus of apartheid control. The budget was passed by the committee and sent to the governor's desk.

While the budget was being hashed out that year, a Republican state senator had submitted a provision that would have prevented family planning funds from going to any group that promoted or provided abortions. The target, as it so often is, was Planned Parenthood. In negotiations, this provision was stricken by Democratic legislators, but a State Senate staff member failed to remove it before it was sent to the Republican governor. It was understood that he would veto it, acknowledging that it was not supposed to have been sent to him at all. Instead, in a shocking turn, he kept it in. What Governor George Deukmejian did veto, however, was Assemblywoman Waters's plan for divestment from South African companies. The legislators were outraged at the governor's editorializing on both counts, but were, at first, powerless against him. With his veto, Deukmejian wrote, "I have concluded that the state budget is not the appropriate instrument in which to express our abhorrence of apartheid and our advice to the fiduciaries of state pension funds." This was infuriating, particularly since the antiabortion provision that hadn't even been legally included was on its way to becoming set policy and affecting the lives of millions of Californians. The budget wasn't the place to address grave human rights abuse and systemic oppression, but was the place to have a partisan debate about women's health? Her plan for the budget effectively stanched, Maxine Waters had a new target: the governor himself.

WINDOW DRESSING

Deukmejian was in favor of a proposed repeal of the state's unitary tax, which taxed corporations on the basis of worldwide income, rather than on income generated in California. Having made it through some initial challenges in the spring of 1985, the bill passed the State Senate before encountering one final hurdle: the assemblywoman from the 48th District. Supported by her Democratic counterparts, Waters drafted an amendment to the corporate tax break bill that would require those corporations who received the benefit to—see if you can guess—divest from South Africa. Republicans balked. The Democrats held fast. If the governor wanted the bill, and he did want it, the amendment would have to go through. Assembly Speaker Willie Brown, Waters's steadfast ally, said the divestment amendment was "key" to the bill's passage; there would be no other way.

Meanwhile, at the national level, wheels were beginning to turn. In September 1985, President Ronald Reagan levied sanctions on South Africa in protest against apartheid. The sanctions applied largely to private trade, however, and were not as comprehensive as full divestiture. For many, including Waters, it wasn't enough. Years later, looking back on the time, she would revisit the deep outrage she felt at Reagan's weak stance. American companies that did business in South Africa could see how their black workers lived there, how the apartheid government treated them, she said in an interview with Katie Couric. "That moved me to say no. This is not right. These American companies cannot be there basically siding with the apartheid government."

Deukmejian and Waters still did not see eye to eye. He vetoed the unitary tax repeal bill, despite being in favor of it, and took a Reagan-like approach of proposing an executive order asking pension officers to review their investments, which is very much not the same thing. Waters wasn't satisfied. She and Deukmejian had a private meeting in which they continued to debate the issue. For Waters, his proposed sanctions weren't tough enough and didn't go far enough. The executive order was little more than window dressing to her. "It simply requests pension fund managers to take a look at the companies and see if they are being good corporate citizens," she told the *Los Angeles Times.* This was not the same as forcing them to divest. And, for a bill that stood to deliver $258 million in tax breaks to some of the world's largest corporations, it was not unreasonable to ask for something more in return. "I think it's very relevant to be able to say that if you get this tax break, we are going to ensure that there are going to be no new investments in South Africa," she concluded.

The governor and the assemblywoman remained at an impasse; the bill died. In an ironic development, by February 1986, Reagan, the former governor of California, had been moved to voice his support for the repeal of a unitary tax. He was trying to keep the peace with British prime minister Margaret Thatcher, who had been given the power by Parliament to punish any U.S. corporations that were headquartered in a state with a unitary tax, as a protest for the initiative as a whole. It seems, then, that a foreign government's actions in relation to private corporations could actually affect national politics and spur leaders to move. Just what Waters had been saying vis-à-vis South Africa all along. Wonder what the difference was . . .

Elsewhere, the anti-apartheid movement was growing, and the power of economic action was being harnessed against the South African government. In 1986, the Presbyterian Church divested its investments from the country; the Cities of Los Angeles and West Hollywood did as well. The University of California Board of Regents, which had been resistant for years, voted to sell $12.3 million in stock. By this time, Deukmejian was in a tough reelection race against Los Angeles mayor Tom Bradley, who'd been one of the state's most fervent anti-apartheid advocates. A California Republican lawmaker drafted a new bill to repeal the state's unitary tax, but Democrats would not support it without a divestiture amendment. The governor was moved to call a private conference with Waters and Brown to discuss a change in his stance. After years of stalemates and a decisive veto, the governor finally wanted to act on South Africa. "California cannot ignore the deteriorating situation in that country," he later said. "We must not turn our backs on black South Africans at this moment of great crisis." While grateful for his change of heart, Waters understood what brought it about. "I think a lot of it was political. He didn't want the embarrassment of it," she told the *New York Times*.

After the governor's conference with Waters and Brown, things moved very quickly on a new proposal for divestment that would require state pensions and the University of California to sell more than $11 billion in South Africa–related stocks. It was larger than any other action in the United States. Waters was elated and, after years of work, vindicated. "The state of California will send an important signal out across this country and out across the world that we are no longer going to do business with firms that help to prop up a regime that has apartheid, a government where racism is constitutionally enshrined." After giving final approval to the bill, the members of the California Assembly took an extraordinary additional step. They stood as one to applaud the steadfast work of Maxine Waters, who had, for years, been tirelessly campaigning, strategizing, speaking out, and, when the situation demanded it, sitting in, to strike a blow for freedom for her people in South Africa.

Maxine and Sidney

Chances are, if Maxine Waters is stunting on a red carpet somewhere, one man will always be just an arm's length away. He's the tall drink of water looking Samuel L. Jackson–fine in a dark suit and bow tie. We're talking about her second husband and lifelong partner in couple's goals, Sidney Williams.

Maxine and Sidney met in the mid-1970s in Councilman David S. Cunningham's office, where Williams served as a staffer from 1974 to 1976. At Cunningham's funeral in 2017, the congresswoman offered up some rare insight into the couple's meet-cute. "She talked about how when Sidney came in she saw him and said, 'I need to meet *him*,' and the next thing you know . . ." Rick Taylor, Waters's former campaign aide, recalled. Sidney, then thirty-five, and Maxine, thirty-nine, were married in 1977, not long after Waters won her Assembly seat in Sacramento. So while she was fighting to represent the folks of South Central L.A., Waters was also finding love. Talk about multitasking. "They have a phenomenal bond," Taylor added. "Most marriages would love to have that kind of relationship. They trust each other. They work together. They really are a team."

One thing that might make their five decades and counting relationship work? Williams, a former linebacker for the Cleveland Browns, sales executive for Mercedes-Benz, and ambassador to the Bahamas, is a fan of his wife. "I have my career and she has hers," said Williams in an *Ebony* magazine interview. "I'm an ex-professional football player. So all the accolades she's getting right now, I've gone through. So it's not a big deal. It's her time to be the shining light. I admire her for that. She has worked very hard to be in the position that she's in right now. I enjoy every minute of it that she's happy."

Sidney Williams and Maxine Waters.

CHAPTER FIVE

UPRISING

1990–1993

IN WHICH WE LEARN HOW VIOLENT PROTESTS
IN REPRESENTATIVE WATERS'S DISTRICT THRUST
HER INTO THE NATIONAL SPOTLIGHT

ompared to the absolute scandal that surrounded Assembly-man Leon Ralph's retirement and Maxine Waters's dramatic debut into elected office, her ascent from the Assembly to the U.S. House of Representatives was essentially by the book. There was no last-minute filing, no furious call to the secretary of state, no mad scramble. When eighty-two-year-old Representative Augustus F. Hawkins, the first black person ever sent to Congress from the West, announced in January 1990 that he would not seek reelection, there was hardly any drama at all. In the end, it all boiled down to a phone call.

Before announcing his retirement, Hawkins phoned Waters to let her know about his plan. This was not a surprise. Waters had long been expected to run for, and presumably win, the 29th District seat after Hawkins vacated it. The question was just when. By the time the moment arrived, Waters had logged fourteen years in the Assembly and Hawkins had put in twice that number in Congress. She was, by many accounts, his heir apparent—a passionate defender of civil rights, supporter of education, and advocate for fair housing. Hawkins called Waters on a Friday morning in January and announced his decision via press release later that afternoon; by evening she had declared her intention to run.

Despite their shared values, Waters and the long-serving congressman couldn't have been more different in approach. The president of the Los Angeles chapter of the Urban League, John Mack, said of Hawkins, "He was not the charismatic kind of speechmaker that some others may have been but he was a doer." Waters was a doer, of course, but part of her process of doing was speaking things into existence, using the power and poetry and precision of her words to catch people's attention and compel them to act. While the handoff between the two powerful black Californians was relatively simple,

Waters didn't simply accept her new, more powerful position as a given. She intended to win the election to Congress by winning over both the establishment and her constituents. At age fifty-one, Waters brought the same truth-telling, take-no-prisoners energy to this new phase that she had to the previous decade and a half. When asked by the *Los Angeles Times* if she expected competitors for Hawkins's old seat, she blithely replied, "There are no obvious ones."

Look, it's not bragging if it's true. By the end of the 1980s, Waters had a proven track record in the Assembly, the loyalty of voters and donors, and alliances with, among others, Jesse Jackson, Los Angeles mayor Tom Bradley, and Speaker of the Assembly Willie L. Brown Jr., who would later become mayor of San Francisco. She'd scored a major victory with her anti-apartheid work and had successfully fought to get affirmative action amendments into a $560 million spending bill, requiring the state to place 15 percent of its contracts with minority-owned businesses. She'd become the first woman to head the California Assembly Democratic Caucus, had been floated as a possible VP running mate for Walter Mondale, and had been declared by *Ebony* "America's Most Influential Black Woman Politician." The idea that it was her time was undoubtable. Every wristwatch said it was her time. Even sundials were declaring "Maxine O'Clock!"

Rosa Parks speaks at a rally of Waters's first congressional campaign.

Despite having Hawkins's blessing and being the obvious front-runner, Waters put in the work to reach Election Day. Instead of taking it easy, she rallied her supporters and raised funds to the tune of $40,000; she pounded the pavement of her district and gave five to six speeches every day in the weeks leading up to the primary. She ran the race like she had something to prove. And her competition? Three men with not even a fraction of her track record: a Larouche Democrat, a Democrat who'd run for office twice as a Republican, and a political novice running his campaign out of a barbecue restaurant. The two-time Republican, by the by, said he'd switched parties only to gain "intelligence" on the opposition. Truly. Sheesh. Maxine Waters pulling out all the stops against this crew was a bit like Flo-Jo strapping on her Nikes and running the hundred-meter dash against a crew of leisurely sloths.

In the primary on June 6, 1990, 34,075 people cast their ballots for Maxine Waters, accounting for 89 percent of the votes. Like she said, there were no obvious competitors. In the general election the following November, the number of ballots cast for her rose to 48,769, good enough for 80 percent of the vote and a decisive victory. That night, at the Biltmore Hotel, she accepted the public's mandate in front of hundreds of supporters. "I'm going to do what I've always done," she said. "I'm going to be a voice for the people who sent me."

On that Friday morning the previous January, when Augustus Hawkins had rung up Maxine Waters, passed the baton, and started the clock on her tenure, it was clear that she would continue to fight for her people. But what neither leader could have predicted was how a series of escalating local events would soon shape that fight, amplify her voice, and change the nation.

BLACK RIBBON

"We're not jumping up and down enough!" Maxine Waters cried out from the pulpit of a Compton Baptist church on Martin Luther King Jr. Day in 1989. "It's not enough to talk about gangs, drugs, and unemployment. . . . What have you done lately?" Shouts of affirmation sprang up from the crowd; it may have been Monday, but this was still church, and Maxine was preaching. "I yearn for the old days, when we were not socialized by someone else's definition of what diplomacy is, when we were not too cute to make some noise!"

It's easy to read her words as prophecy, coming three years before the spark of the verdict in the Rodney King beating trial would ignite the tinder of economic isolation, systemic oppression, and frustration in South Central. But this has also been Maxine Waters's thesis for years. It was not that she would be proven right about the intersecting issues facing her community because of the violence that shook Los Angeles in 1992; violence shook Los Angeles in 1992 *because* she was right.

Waters outside the U.S. Capitol, 1995.

Back on that MLK Day in 1989, just a few hours after Waters's speech at the pulpit in Compton, a car was pulled over while traveling down the Pacific Coast Highway near Martin Luther King Jr. Avenue. See, as through grainy dash camera footage, two white police officers stop a sedan driven by two black men. Though the officers would later claim the black men's car was weaving, a covert videotape of the stop would not bear that out. What it did show, however, was one of the officers shoving the face of one of the black men through a window and then launching him onto the trunk of the police car.

It was merely one incident in a pattern of police brutality that California representative Don Edwards would later call an epidemic.

The only thing that made the stop on January 14, 1989, stand out—and, in a dark echo two years and two months later, would make a similar attack on a man named Rodney King stand out—was videotape.

The driver, a man named Diop Kamau, who was then going by the name Don Jackson, was a Hawthorne police sergeant; his passenger, Jeff Hill, was an off-duty federal corrections officer; and the camera, secreted in a van that was trailing Kamau's car, belonged to NBC. And the whole incident came about because of Kamau's educated guess based on the sad realities of being black in Los Angeles.

After years of putting up with racist behavior from fellow police officers, including lynching photos posted at police headquarters, and culminating with a traffic stop during which his own father, a veteran of the Los Angeles Sheriff's Department, was pulled from his vehicle and beaten by police officers, Kamau had reached a breaking point. On leave from the department (a police psychiatrist would diagnose him as "hypersensitive to racism"), Kamau had embarked on a second career in the law and order field. Convinced that police in California were pulling over black motorists at an inordinately higher rate than motorists of other races, and that those stops often resulted in excessive force and violence, Kamau devised a plan to catch officers in the act, with himself as the bait. The premise was infuriatingly simple: Kamau, a black man, would simply drive around—sometimes in a beat-up rented car—and wait to be pulled over. And when he saw another person being stopped by the police, he'd also stop to bear witness. And he always had a camera at the ready to record anecdotal evidence for his litmus test of the department and the individuals in it. By the time of the MLK Day incident, Kamau estimates that he'd stopped to witness or been stopped himself three hundred times. Though most of the interactions he'd caught on camera were unremarkable, his crusade captured the attention of producers from NBC's news division, which sent out a crew to follow one of Kamau's stakeouts.

By this time, Kamau's vigilante tactics were well-known among California police departments and largely reviled as unduly antagonistic. He described himself as the product of a four-hundred-year-old battle between the police and African Americans. For the sergeant, the moral truth at the center was simple: "You can't bait a good cop."

The videotaped stop that ended with Kamau being smashed through a window set off a flurry of activity. In a news culture that was stretching perilously close to the twenty-four-hour cycle in which we now live, the media grabbed the video and played it over and over again for days across the nation. Reporters jumped on the story of the cop who sought justice for his own brothers. Critics called Kamau's actions a provocative ambush; supporters countered that the only provocation was making public what had long been covert. The FBI and the Los Angeles County district attorney investigated, while op-ed pages hemmed and hawed over whether it was evidence of a pattern or an isolated occurrence. As the country grappled with the Rodney King beating two years later, it often seemed that the lived experience of being black in America was up for debate.

For Assemblywoman Maxine Waters, and many other black Americans, the debate was focusing on all the wrong premises. Waters regarded Kamau and Hill as heroes. "No one ever documented racism in the police before," she told *People* magazine. So supportive was she that, along with Representative Hawkins and Dionne Warwick, she organized a fund-raiser at the Hollywood Roosevelt Hotel to support Kamau; it was attended by Marla Gibbs, of *The Jeffersons* and *227*, and former NFLer Jim Brown, among others. This was in March 1989, two months after the traffic stop, as the investigation escalated and soon after the arresting officer, Mark Dickey, admitted to a State Senate oversight committee that his official report contained falsehoods that he attributed to "a faulty memory." In the spring of 1989, the charges against Kamau were dropped and misdemeanor charges against the two officers were filed. In August, the Long Beach City Council voted to put a proposal for a Citizen Police Complaint Commission on the ballot. In November 1990, the two officers, then ages twenty-nine and twenty-eight, received stress-related disability retirements from the Long Beach Police Department. And on March 4, 1991, the day after George Holliday filmed uniformed members of the Los Angeles Police Department savagely beating Rodney King on California State Route 210, the trial of the Long Beach officers began. The trial ended with a mistrial and a dismissal of charges against the officers.

"When it happened," Maxine Waters would say of the Los Angeles insurrection twenty-five years after the fact, "it was almost as if I knew something was going to give." For decades, she had been one of the only voices calling out the injustice that weighed down and cut short the lives of those in her district. For thousands of South Central residents, something had already given in their support systems, their prospects, their connection to hope. Little cracks in a wall that was about to come tumbling down.

The first time, of dozens, she saw the video footage of Rodney King's beating, Waters was out of town on business. "Oh my god! Oh my god!" she cried out in her hotel room as the grainy low-color video played on cable news. No matter how many times you've seen it in the intervening years, the footage remains shocking in its brutality and its relentlessness. It's remarkable, then, to remember that Lake View Terrace resident George Holliday, the cameraman, didn't even realize what he'd captured until he played it back on his VCR.

He was just trying to capture "a bit of action" with a new camcorder from the second floor of the Mountain Back Apartments. Instead, what he got was graphic footage of officers kicking and beating King with baton blows known as "power strokes," as King struggled to pull himself off the ground, Taser wires still biting into his skin.

When all was said and done, King had been Tasered, kicked repeatedly, and given fifty-six power strokes before being dragged on his stomach to the gutter. Though only three officers are seen attacking King in the video, there were seventeen Los Angeles police officers from various divisions gathered around one traffic stop. Right before beginning their attack on King, two officers had sent a computer message about a domestic dispute in which they intervened earlier between a black couple. In the message, the officers had said the couple was "right out of *Gorillas in the Mist*."

Initially, the reports from the officers involved downplayed what actually occurred. Officer Laurence M. Powell, one of the men in the video, would write:

> *Deft recovered almost immediately [from the effects of the Taser] and resumed his hostile charge in our direction. Ofcr Wind and I drew our batons to defend against deft's attack and struck him several times in the arm and leg areas to incapacitate him. Deft. continued resisting kicking and swinging his arms at us. We finally kicked deft down and he was subdued by several ofcrs using the swarm technique.*

This would have been the official line if not for Holliday's video. "Perhaps the greatest single barrier to the effective investigation and adjudication is the officers' unwritten code of silence," the Independent Commission on the Los Angeles Police Department later claimed; "an officer does not provide adverse information against a fellow officer." The morning after the beating, George Holliday called his local precinct and reported that he'd witnessed an instance of police brutality. The desk officer did not ask him any follow-up questions and no complaint was generated. That same day, King's brother also tried to report the use of excessive force but got nowhere. Meanwhile, King was hospitalized, suffering from a fractured eye socket, a broken cheekbone, a broken leg, bruises, facial nerve damage, a severe concussion, and Taser burns.

After being rebuffed by the LAPD, Holliday then contacted Los Angeles television station KTLA. They purchased the footage for five hundred dollars and began broadcasting it that night. It was picked up by CNN the following morning and spread like wildfire across the nation and into Maxine Waters's hotel room.

After the footage aired, Police Chief Daryl Gates denounced the beating but called it "an aberration." Waters countered, "This is the order of the day in Los Angeles." Years of anecdotal evidence sided with Waters. To wit, a poll conducted by the *Los Angeles Times* days after the video began airing found that 63 percent of respondents in the city of Los Angeles "believed incidents of police brutality involving the LAPD are common." A later survey of 960 LAPD officers by the Independent Commission, commonly referred to as the Christopher Commission after commission head Warren Christopher, found that 27.6 percent of respondents "agreed that 'an officer's prejudice towards the suspect's race may lead to the use of excessive force.'" "It is apparent," the commission found, "that too many LAPD patrol officers view citizens with resentment and hostility."

Gates held a press conference at which he expressed a very conditional contrition. "He's on parole," he said of King. "He's a convicted robber. In spite of the fact that he's on parole and a convicted robber, I'd be glad to apologize. He did not deserve that beating. We are ashamed of the fact that he got that beating and no question about it, he deserves an apology or more." What Gates did not realize was that the dam was breaking all around him and that supercilious half-apologies for blatant atrocities weren't ever good enough.

A SECOND WATTS REVOLUTION

The block, as they say, was hot, even months before violence erupted in South Central. The furor over the Rodney King beating carried into the summer of 1991, even after four of the officers involved were indicted. Maxine Waters, who had squared off with Gates before, wanted more than the indictment. She joined other black leaders, including Mayor Tom Bradley, in calling for Gates's resignation. The commission report, released in July 1991, also recommended he be replaced. City council president John Ferraro put out a call for black leaders to "lower the rhetoric" as he tried to negotiate Gates's exit. Waters wasn't trying to hear that. She informed Ferraro that she had every intention of showing up at the next council meeting to "lambaste" Gates. So afraid of her were they that they locked the doors and adjourned early. It didn't much matter: Gates announced his retirement days later, setting a departure date of April 1992.

Though Waters was now ensconced in Washington, D.C., events in her district kept her focus. The problems she had talked about for years hadn't quieted down. If anything, they were getting louder. One week after the King beating, for instance, a riot had broken out at a Westwood movie theater prior to an oversold screening of *New Jack City*. For three hours, people dumped trash cans and jumped on the hoods of cars. Witnesses and police linked the violence to anger over the King video, which continued to be replayed on television, and the ongoing issue of police brutality. An eighteen-year-old Ava DuVernay, then a student at the University of California, Los

Angeles, and a witness to the Westwood riot, surmised that if the police had tried to intervene more than they had, it would have set off the powder keg. It "would have been a Watts revolution," she told the *Los Angeles Times*. DuVernay would go on to become the first black woman to be nominated for a Golden Globe for Best Director and the first black woman to have a film nominated for Best Picture, for her movie *Selma*. She would also direct the acclaimed film *13th* and the award-winning miniseries *When They See Us,* both of which focus on the effects of institutional racism and corruption in the criminal justice system on black people.

In November 1991, during a blackout at the Imperial Courts housing project, police responded to a report of shots fired. They exchanged fire with and eventually killed a man named Henry Peco. Many residents claimed Peco had been unarmed, and a crowd of more than one hundred took to the streets around the project to demand an investigation. Gates held a press conference and claimed that Peco was found to have gunpowder residue on his hands, but Waters wasn't mollified because the people weren't mollified. "The people there are angry, upset, and frightened," she told the Police Commission a week later. "We're on the verge of a holocaust in Los Angeles."

On Christmas Eve, a police car ran over a shrine to Peco at Imperial Courts during a chase, further escalating tensions between residents and the police. On December 30, a police sweep of Imperial Courts resulted in forty-four arrests for outstanding warrants and further angered residents. On New Year's Eve of 1991, Representative Waters toured Imperial Courts herself. She wanted, she said, to "make sure the police know you are not alone—that we are here with you." She left one resident with two video cameras to record any future incidents. "The police need to be watched," she said.

On January 14, 1992, Waters brought twenty Imperial Courts residents to testify in front of the Los Angeles Police Commission about the uptick in police harassment in the wake of Peco's killing. She brought with her a thirteen-year-old girl who had been at Imperial Courts the night of the shooting. "The police grabbed me and called me a little bitch," the girl said. "Right now I'm afraid to protest because I'm afraid of the LAPD." Waters stood to address the commission. "We have nowhere else to go," she said. "Please call off the dogs."

On March 5, 1992, opening statements for the trial of four of the officers who beat King began in Simi Valley, a predominantly white city in Ventura County, after the defense had won a change of venue. Ten white people, one Latinx person, and one Asian person sat on the jury. Sergeant Stacey C. Koon and Officers Laurence M. Powell, Theodore J. Briseno, and Timothy E. Wind were charged with felony assault and excessive force. After seven days of deliberations, on April 29, the jury acquitted all four of assault and all but Powell of excessive force. On Powell, they could not come to a consensus and a mistrial on that count of excessive force was declared. It was later revealed that the not-guilty verdicts had been reached after only six hours of deliberation. In the hours after the verdict was announced in Simi Valley, the thing that had been holding back the dam in Los Angeles finally gave way and broke.

"WHAT DID YOU EXPECT?"

Mere hours had passed since the verdict was announced, and yet there was already broken glass at the corner of Florence and Normandie Avenues. Like whispered gossip, the ever-present frustration was elevated by the verdict and spread through the streets and stores of South Central, and violence and fires erupted as people started looting. Lights flickered and went out as walls of flames rose up. Though the insurrection spread, the people of South Central couldn't get out, hemmed in by power outages and highways and, eventually, National Guardsmen. Just as a year before, when the images of Rodney King's beating took over the airwaves, now the sight of Los Angeles burning played from coast to coast, morning until night.

By the end of the first night, Waters, Bradley, and Jesse Jackson were among those trying to mitigate the crisis by focusing on root causes. While President George H. W. Bush issued statements decrying "lawlessness," Waters and Jackson urged William P. Barr, then the U.S. attorney general and, coincidentally, the author of the 1992 report *The Case for More Incarceration,* to bring federal charges against the policemen for violating King's civil rights. Before the sun had set on the first full day of the insurrection, it was clear that two very different narratives were forming. Arthur Fletcher, the black chairman of the U.S. Commission on Civil Rights, said the issue was "a cancer of racism that's been eating away at the nation's moral fiber and infiltrating and infecting practically every major institution in government, education, health—and the judicial system, the cornerstone of our democracy." Bush, on the other hand, characterized the insurrection as "wanton destruction." "We simply cannot condone violence as a way of changing the system," he said. Waters told the press on the morning after the fires started,

> *Let's be straight about this, we have no access to the White House. We had one meeting since I have been in Congress with the President. It was pro forma, it was courtesy, but there is no relationship. . . . I think that immediately we need an indication from the POTUS that he is encouraging his Justice Department to prosecute. . . . We're asking him to use leadership to say to this nation that he believes that there has been injustice. And we're asking him to speak directly to the*

young black males and tell them that their lives are valuable in this country.

The second day of the insurrection was a Thursday, which in 1992 also meant Must See TV on NBC for most of America: *A Different World, Cheers, Wings,* and, in its final season, *The Cosby Show.* Bill Cosby, in New York City, watched Maxine Waters talk to Katie Couric on the *Today* show that morning as he tried to figure out how he could be of assistance. Already, Waters's message stood in stark contrast to the president's. And, it would turn out, to Cosby's. "I'm very pained by the fact that people's anger has spilled over into the streets," Waters said before adding, crucially, "I understand the anger, however. I'm just as angry as they are. I think we had an opportunity to avoid this."

Cosby reached out to Mayor Bradley and asked for his advice. Cosby wanted to record a message to play either before the broadcast of the series finale of his show or, if the local NBC affiliate, KNBC, opted not to interrupt insurrection coverage, in its stead. Bradley gave his advice and Cosby headed into the studio. That night, KNBC decided to play the anticipated broadcast as well as Cosby's message. "Today Mayor Bradley urged us to stay home," anchor Jess Marlow said at the top of the 8 P.M. hour. "Stay off the streets and watch *The Cosby Show.* We believe we need this time [as] a cooling-off period." This specific language of cooling off would recur through the following days, often in opposition to Waters's understanding of the events, which were, simply put, that the people had a right to be angry, to stay hot.

This was, unsurprisingly, something of a tough sell to the country's most powerful. To hear the president speak, this was a breakdown of society at the most basic level. And even though in the insurrection, it's well documented that people of all races engaged in violence and looted, it's hard not to understand Bush's words, and the predominant narrative around lawlessness and mob brutality, through a racialized lens. Simply put, in Los Angeles, black people had gone wild. And so a special message from Cosby, then the patron saint of black respectability, seems in retrospect almost too perfect an antidote. "Let us all pray that everyone from the top of the government down to the people in the streets . . . would all have good sense," he said in his video message. "And let us pray for a better tomorrow, which starts today."

The insurrection would continue for another day and a half. Meanwhile, 45 percent of the country's viewing audience tuned in to say farewell to the Huxtable family.

The flames in Los Angeles storefronts on millions of screens giving away to the fictional world of the tidy living room and the cultured artwork and the loving quips of a well-to-do black family must have been jarring at the time. Now, in the present, the juxtaposition is almost too heavily symbolic to even consider. The idea of TV executives debating whether to cut away from the images of an American city burning to broadcast the laugh-tracked end of a halcyon era in black representation? If it were fiction, it would be unreadable. And then to add to that the post-show legacy of its star, the way the veneer of respectability would crack and dissolve until, twenty-five years later, a seemingly unimpeachable moral voice of (a certain type of) black America sat in a jail cell. Suffice it all to say, the story of the past is always more complex than it seems.

Elsewhere in America, Bill Clinton, campaigning for president, laid the blame for the violence squarely at the feet of the Republican Party, who he said had abandoned the black community in the Reagan and Bush years by cutting back on urban revitalization programs and using strategic dog whistles—like the 1988 television commercial featuring convicted murderer Willie Horton—to win over the parties' more prejudiced sides. While Bush spoke of lawlessness, Clinton, advised by Waters, found a message somewhat closer to equanimity. The people of South Central were looting "because they are not part of the system at all anymore," he cried out during a speech in New Orleans, the night before flying to Los Angeles. "They do not share our values, and their children are growing up in a culture alien from ours, without family, without neighborhood, without church, without support." While the us-and-them rhetoric still reflects the sensibilities of a predominant culture resistant to the idea that the people they were seeing on television were both Americans and actual people, it is worlds away from Bush's framing.

This is the same sort of distancing that occurred after the Watts riots, a pervasive idea that there was another America where this was happening. While the lived experience of people in Watts and elsewhere in South Central in the 1990s surely felt like another world than the one on television or on the cover of *Ebony,* it was constantly being impeded, invaded, and oppressed by the "main" world. This was Maxine Waters's point: this other world is our world; we cannot abandon it. Clinton would go on to tour Los Angeles with Waters and later meet with black community leaders at her home, but still, in public remarks he toed the us-and-them line. Having spoken about "personal responsibility" and "the disintegration of family" among L.A.'s poor black populations in other cities while the insurrection was happening, he toned it down a bit but still ended up referring to those who committed violent acts as hoodlums, while in Waters's home, it was a term that chafed those gathered.

Waters, meanwhile, had spent the days of violence and chaos in the streets, trying to help her people. She'd come straight to a Los Angeles public housing project in her district after the insurrection began. There, in the dark, on a street where the lights had gone out, she began the work that would occupy her for the next week: she wanted to get supplies to people who needed it, food for kids, diapers for babies. The substance of survival. She said in a 2017 interview, looking back on that time:

> *I'd get up early in the morning, [I would] go to the TV stations trying to explain to them the difference between rioting and people who've been dropped off of America's agenda and find themselves in a situation where the kids are hungry and the place is burning and at that time, everybody was being seen as a "robber" and a "thug" and someone who was responsible for the burning. . . . What I tried to do was take it out of the discussion of "these are just no good, crazy rioting people" and to talk about what I call an insurrection, which made a lot of white people mad.*

Waters and President Bill Clinton tour South Central Los Angeles on May 4, 1992.

Waters became a leading, if publicly dissenting, voice in the conversation around the Los Angeles insurrection. "What did you expect?" she asked when pressed for a reaction to the verdict in the case of Rodney King's assailants. And, really, what more was there to say? She'd been making her case for years; the people of her district had been making their case for years. What did anyone expect? Time and again she was pushed to condemn the people who looted. Time and again she refused, pulling the focus wider to the causes of the looting. When her own local offices were burned to the ground, she remained on message, saying she wasn't angry at all. The offices were, as she explained in the *Los Angeles Times*, "just one of the victims of the rebellion." To bolster her view of the events after the verdict,

Waters urged leaders like Tom Bradley to stop calling it a riot, arguing that that language trapped her constituents in a linguistic vise—it was impossible for people to see a riot as a just response and to see rioters as anything other than criminals. She preferred the phrase "L.A. insurrection"; she pushed back against "L.A. riot" at every opportunity. The day after violence broke out, she held a press conference with the Congressional Black Caucus in the U.S. Capitol. She delivered remarks that would come to define her place in this moment in history and would connect the work she had done in her entire career to the extraordinary events happening in her district. It's foolish to try to boil down a politician's outlook to a simple thesis, but if you did you could do worse than the words she delivered in a clear, forceful voice at that podium:

> *There are those who would like for me and others and all of us to tell people to go inside, to be peaceful, that they have to accept the verdict. I accept the responsibility of asking people not to endanger their lives. I am not asking people not to be angry. I am angry and I have a right to that anger and the people out there have a right to that anger. . . . There are some angry people in America, and young black males in my district are feeling, at this moment, if they could not get a conviction with the Rodney King video available to the jurors, that there can be no justice in America.*

"I KNOW HOW TO TALK TO MY PEOPLE"

On Tuesday, April 13, 1993, almost a year after the insurrection roared through Los Angeles, Maxine Waters stood on the corner of Vermont and Manchester in South Central. Around her, buildings were slowly being rebuilt, some businesses had reopened, the lights were back on. Life had, in some ways, gone on. But she was afraid that all of that, cold comfort though it might have been, would come to a halt again. The civil trial of the officers who'd been acquitted of criminal charges was coming to a close. Waters, and many others in the community, feared that if justice was again denied, the city would once again break into chaos and violence. Maxine Waters had a plan to prevent that. She and her staff gathered on that afternoon, preparing to hand out 350,000 copies of a letter she'd written specifically to the people she represented. She addressed the residents of South Central, her constituents, as "my dear children." She urged them, no matter what the verdict in the civil trial of Koon, Powell, Wind, and Briseno, to keep their eyes on the prize. "This Rodney King thing is a mother!" the letter exclaimed, making use of her unique ability to speak with a unifying and familiar voice. "We must let the world know we are not going anywhere. This is our city and our community. We have got to make it right." She talked again, always, about jobs and justice in the same breath. How she struggled to usher her community into a new day, with or without the support of the system. "Each day brings a new opportunity, a new possibility," she wrote in closing. "I love you and will fight for you. I need you to stand with me to make this a better place." In an extraordinary gesture, a sitting congresswoman walked through her district and passed out hundreds of thousands of letters in which she declared, "We have got to live!"

The Presidents

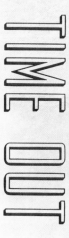

The relationship between a member of Congress and a president can be an ever-shifting, ever-evolving one. At times there are compromises to be made for crucial legislation; at others there are hard lines to be drawn, ensuring that the separate branches of government keep each other in check. This is how it always goes, and the tenure of Representative Maxine Waters has been no exception. However, true to her signature style, Waters's interactions with sitting presidents—positive, negative, and everything in between—have never been boring. While the battle royale she waged against President Donald Trump may be the first to spring to mind, she has been going toe-to-toe with the White House over what she believes in her entire career. Let's take a look back at some notable moments.

PRESIDENT GEORGE H. W. BUSH

In May 1992, right after the uprising in Los Angeles, Maxine Waters was at a black town hall being covered by reporter Ted Koppel of *Nightline*. An audience member implored Koppel, a venerated white news anchor, to use his influence to convince President George H. W. Bush to help the people of Los Angeles. Waters interjected before Koppel could respond and set the record straight: "I don't ever want to hear you say that one little white man has more power to get things done than you do!" she said. And if there is ever a lens to consider Waters's relationship to Bush, and to the office of the president in general, it's that. Yes, he was the president, but to her he was also one little white man and the people had the power.

Considering that Waters brought that level of energy into a town hall, you can only imagine how much more forceful she was, and is, in the halls of Congress and the White House. It's not a good idea to ignore Maxine

Waters. Now, this is true no matter who you are or what your station is in life. President, pope, private citizen: it's best practice to look alive and listen up when Maxine Waters is speaking. Many men, overestimating their power or underestimating hers—or both—have failed to give the legislator her due. But, like the IRS on tax day, Waters is quick to let them know it's time to pay up. Never one to shy away from speaking her mind, she has, over the years, had to put all manner of men in their places, from private citizens to presidents. (The pope, heretofore, has remained in her good graces. Will update if this changes.) You can find such instances all the way back in her assemblywoman days, but—as we move away from the L.A. insurrection and enter the Clinton era—let's get into Maxine Waters's decisive dressings down of a father and a son who, at different points, were the most powerful men in the world—and still they were no match for the congresswoman from Southern California.

It was probably never in the cards for George H. W. Bush and Maxine Waters to see eye to eye. Prior to her election to Congress, she did double duty as an assemblywoman and a surrogate for Jesse Jackson's 1984 presidential campaign, seeking to make Ronald Reagan and Bush, his vice president, one-termers. There's an alternate universe somewhere in which, during the lead-up to that election, Maxine Waters faced off against George H. W. Bush in a vice presidential debate. Here's how it could have happened: Jackson was making the first of two runs for president on a very liberal platform that included reparations for descendants of enslaved people, resistance to the apartheid government of South Africa, and the ratification of the Equal Rights Amendment, among other items. Waters was seen as one of the most left-leaning members of Jackson's coalition. While Jackson did better than some pundits predicted at the 1984 Democratic National Convention, Walter Mondale became the nominee, facing off against the incumbent Reagan-Bush ticket. Prior to the convention, Jackson met with Mondale in Kansas City, where both were addressing the NAACP, and gave him a list of

RECLAIMING HER TIME

potential vice presidential picks. Included on that list was Maxine Waters. While Mondale never formally approached Waters about the ticket, she had an answer ready. She told a gathering of Alpha Kappa Alphas that year that, had Mondale asked her, she would have informed him, "I don't have time to play games." As she would later prove as an adviser for the Dukakis campaign, she did not come to pretend she was moving the party in a more liberal direction. If she was joining a ticket, you needed not just to talk about it, but to be about it. Maxine Waters was born being about it. And just imagine, in an alternate universe, her bringing that energy all the way through a convention and onto a debate stage opposite George H. W. Bush, who, in the debate that actually happened, was notoriously patronizing to Democratic vice presidential candidate Geraldine Ferraro. The world would have to wait six years for H.W. and M.W. to end up within sparring range of each other.

A week after the L.A. insurrection began in 1992, H.W., now the president, toured charred shells of buildings in South Central with Secretary of Housing and Urban Development Jack Kemp, Republican senator John Seymour, and Secretary of Health and Human Services Louis Sullivan. It was not going particularly well. It was a real shock that the man who cavalierly threw around the terms "hoodlums" and "wanton lawlessness" and hadn't been particularly popular in the district to begin with wasn't thrown a parade. A mystery. In any case, he wasn't doing much to help himself, either. "We are embarrassed by interracial violence," he told a black Baptist church. A lot is happening in that sentence and yet . . . nothing useful. He promised $300 million in Federal Emergency Management Agency relief for the city, but when pressed about more long-term initiatives, like jobs and education, Bush and Kemp provided what one angry South Central resident

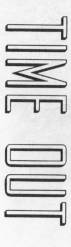

TIME OUT

Waters and Jesse Jackson go way back. Here they sit side by side in 1984.

dismissed as "lip service." In a contentious meeting with five hundred Korean American merchants, lawyer John S. C. Lim told the president, "The federal government's failure and inability to address the oppression felt by African-Americans must be viewed as the cause of the disaster." The quiet part was now being said out loud all around him. Bush listened to the merchants' concerns but warned them, "I can't over-promise; our resources are limited." No one, it seemed, was getting what they needed out of this tour. Or, as Maxine Waters more pointedly put it, the president was a day late and a dollar short. While the president consulted with the mayor of Los Angeles and other community leaders, Waters was noticeably absent from his schedule as Bush rode through her district in a limousine. This infuriated Waters, who had, for days, been walking the streets, standing in line for groceries alongside her constituents, giving voice to the needs of her district on television, and, most of all, listening. "Even though I'm a member of Congress, he won't talk to me," she exclaimed. "How many more rebellions is it going to take, George Bush? You have to stop playing politics."

Playtime, however, would continue for a bit longer, it seemed. Two weeks later, Bush held a meeting with congressional leaders and members of his cabinet to discuss "urban problems" post-insurrection. Somehow, Representative Maxine Waters of California's invitation must have gotten lost in the mail. She was not on the list. But enough was enough; she showed up anyway. "I don't intend to be excluded or dismissed," she told the New York Times. And this time they didn't have the temerity to turn her away.

Throughout the L.A. insurrection and its recovery, Waters was consistent in her intention to redirect questions about black decorum and issues in her district to the powerful places she felt they rightly belonged, namely the systemic oppression that was endemic in America and its leader, George H. W. Bush. She was angry; she'd been angry for a long time. And she knew that she was in the unique position, as a black woman in the House of Representatives, to bring that anger to the seat of power, whether he wanted to hear it or not. She couldn't make him meet her, but he would never escape her voice.

In July 1992, at a National Press Club event, Waters decided that perhaps everyone didn't quite pick up what she was putting down about the president earlier. She'd make it plain how she felt, saying Bush was "a mean-spirited man who has no care or concern about what happens to the African-American community in this country." This is *spicy*. Decades before Kanye West would famously get on a Hurricane Katrina telecast and declare, "George [W.] Bush doesn't care about black people," Maxine Waters was saying the same thing about his father to the press directly. Copyright that! How did this go over with the sitting president? Well, he didn't love it. It's that thing where the worst possible thing that can happen is being called a racist, not, say, having done things that would indicate a lack of care or concern for a particular population. Waters knew she was striking a nerve, but she also, as usual, knew she was speaking the truth as she saw it.

That same month, Bill Clinton accepted the Democratic presidential nomination, which Waters, one of the first established Democrats to publicly endorse Clinton, had seconded from the floor of Madison Square Garden. As in previous elections, Waters was tapped to advise and help stump for the candidate, being made chairwoman of his California campaign. The representative's remarks about the sitting president, naturally, became rich fodder for general election controversy as the GOP tried to tarnish Clinton with Waters's words. This did not go according to plan.

Someone somewhere in the Bush campaign decided, about three weeks later, to make Waters

Waters speaks at the 1992 Democratic National Convention.

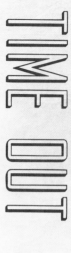

a point of contention and a liability for Clinton. They sent out a press release decrying her remarks to the National Press Club and dispatched then vice president Dan Quayle with similar talking points. At an Ohio rally, he brought up the comments to reporters. "She called George Bush a racist . . . calling him a racist is totally unacceptable." He demanded an apology from the Clinton campaign. This, again, did not go according to plan.

The Clinton campaign responded, essentially, "Yeah . . . no." Spokeswoman Avis LaVelle said, "Bill Clinton is not the parent or guardian of Maxine Waters. . . . If Mr. Quayle wants an apology, he should go to the source of the remark." The Clinton campaign basically told Dan Quayle, "Pull up! See what happens." But, it turned out, Quayle didn't even need to pull up on Maxine Waters; she showed up anyway. This is why you need to keep her name out of your mouth if you're talking foolishness. Two days later, Waters sent a message that completely shut the scandal down. Before a crowd in Inglewood, California, she RSVP'd "No thanks" to the invitation to apologize. "Dan Quayle doesn't know me," she said. "My *mother* couldn't make me do that." Waters was like, "Ms. Velma Lee Moore could not drag this apology out of me, so you know you're out of luck, sir." Truth be told, he should have known not to step to the freshman representative. A year earlier, speculation rose that Bush might replace Quayle on the ticket when he sought reelection. The *Los Angeles Times* reached out to Waters for a comment. And did she disappoint? Honey, does she ever disappoint? She told them that she thought Bush would retain Quayle but that that didn't mean he should. "He is the epitome of the privileged white male who has bypassed the hurdles that the average citizen must overcome in order to achieve position, status or recognition. Yet he dares to oppose affirmative action for women and minorities—many of whom have IQs and training far superior to his—who have been excluded from opportunities." Or, to put it succinctly: "Quayle is a lightweight who makes a mockery of the word 'qualified.'" Waters told you all a long time ago that Dan Quayle was DQ—disqualified—so please, if you're going to try to make her a talking point, get someone who knows what he's talking about.

PRESIDENT BILL CLINTON

"This is the last time I will support a ticket with two white men!" It's 1992 and Maxine Waters is standing in front of a room full of black and brown faces, boldly—and accurately predicting—the future. In the run-up to the presidential election, Waters had been one of the first high-profile black Democrats to throw her support behind Bill Clinton. She had toured Los Angeles with him after the insurrection, and she had been made co-chairwoman of his national steering committee, even as she continued to advise and stump for Jesse Jackson, who was focusing on local elections and had frequently sparred publicly with Clinton. As the two men locked horns, sometimes Waters interceded and sometimes she sat back and let it play out. She wanted to take the White House back for the Democrats and, this one last time, she would concede to two white men—Clinton and running mate Al Gore—being the ones to lead the way. She knew that Clinton's campaign focus was reengaging white voters in the Democratic Party and that a so-called urban agenda might get left by the wayside should he take office. But she also knew that the only way Clinton and Gore were going to get into office was through her, and she was bringing her values with her.

Bill Clinton needed California, which for the first time would have fifty-four electoral votes. He also needed black voters; after striking a centrist tone in response to the insurrection and an unforced error that found him playing golf at a whites-only golf club in Arkansas, things were not going as well as they should have. After the convention, 30 percent of black voters still said they were undecided between Clinton, Bush,

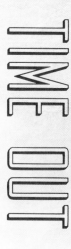

and independent candidate Ross Perot. Less than half of respondents said they were definitely voting for Clinton. "The Democratic Party, in its attempts to get to the White House, and to have to walk this tightrope of not looking too black, too female, too urban, will find that the turnout will not be the kind of turnout—as I look at it today—that may ensure the kind of victory that is anticipated," Waters warned. While she supported his candidacy, she was frank about his potential blind spots and the failures of the Democratic Party in the eyes of the black community. She was not there simply as a figurehead or for political clout; she was there to make change. "Let me tell you where the power really lies," she said. "When a Maxine Waters endorses a Bill Clinton, the power to be at the White House to convince him, to work with him, is an awesome power. . . . I hope he listens to me, I think he does."

November's election, thanks in part to Waters's support, handed California's votes over to Clinton, and would open up new opportunities for Waters to expand her influence. He considered her for HUD secretary; ultimately, she decided she'd be more effective as an independent voice in Congress. But despite their newfound power, the next few years would be anything but smooth sailing for Waters and for Clinton. Scandal plagued Clinton's early appointments and a middle-class tax cut was dropped, despite his promises regarding the same on the campaign trail; his approval rating one hundred days in plummeted to a staggering 37 percent. Waters, however, remained outspoken in support of him, albeit with caveats. "I really do believe that Bill Clinton is more liberal than oftentimes his politics. He's practical. But I think his heart is decent," she said in an interview with the *Los Angeles Times*. "For those of us who understood what was happening politically, we understood that we had very few choices."

Bill Clinton's legacy as president, in the balance, is a subject for another day. What's most worthy of our focus in this moment is the complexity of Maxine Waters's loyalty and the depth of her convictions.

She wasn't, at this time, simply toeing the party line. She would never. But she wasn't flying off the handle for no reason, either. She was, as ever, seeing the big picture, the story behind the story, and doing her job as a legislator accordingly.

PRESIDENT GEORGE W. BUSH

Eight years later, after H.W., his son, George W., would also get off on the wrong foot with Maxine Waters and, truthfully, never regain balance. After the highly contentious election in which Bush won the electoral vote but lost the popular vote and the fate of a nation was briefly and tenuously attached to some hanging chads in Florida, Waters was, to steal a phrase that would become ubiquitous soon thereafter, not ready to make nice. She opted out of attending the inauguration, something she would famously do again for President Trump with much ballyhoo. In 2000, she had simply said, "I will not be healed by that time." Things did not improve.

When George W. Bush, in an effort to mollify the more religious arm of his party, which had grown distrustful of his father, nominated for attorney general John Ashcroft, a religious conservative favorite, Maxine Waters had something to say about it. "Ashcroft represents everything that we know to be harmful to us," she said, referring to his spotty record on civil rights for black Americans, LGBTQ people, and women. Two years later, when the Iraq War began, Waters was vocal about her opposition early, even when the post-9/11 surge in patriotism made that assertion politically risky. She maintained a public criticism of the younger Bush, continually voted against military action, and, in 2005, was one of the cofounders of the Out of Iraq Caucus, aimed at "reining in this president and his misguided policies." When midterm elections flipped the House for the Democrats in 2006, suddenly what was a fringe position became a centrist one and Waters was again in the middle of it. Waters's

House floor statements from this period are especially striking as she clearly, persistently, and unreservedly criticizes the president's decision to stay in Iraq.

Take, for instance, a statement from 2007, after Bush requested an additional $46 billion for war funding. Waters had, of course, been connecting governmental expenditures to the lived experiences of Americans in real and tangible ways since before she was in Congress, and most especially during the insurrection at the tail end of senior Bush's presidency. But she'd gone from a representative who was stunningly ignored by a president visiting her burned-out district to the chair of a caucus that stood between another president and an extended conflict. You could not ignore her.

EXCERPT FROM FLOOR STATEMENT BY MAXINE WATERS, OCTOBER 22, 2007

The President is trying to set us up. He is trying to set us up so that if we don't immediately vote on this $46 billion it will look as if we are not giving the soldiers the necessary equipment in order to wage the war. This is absolutely ridiculous.

And I don't know how long this President thinks he can get along with mismanaging this war in the way that he's doing. We have 101 questions we ought to be forcing on him. First of all, where are the 190,000 weapons that have been lost? Where is the money we were supposed to have been getting from the oil wells in Iraq? Where are the billions of dollars that they sent over in cash in the beginning of this war? What happened to all of that money?

This occupation is draining us, not only the lives of young men and women who are there trying to answer the President's call, but the dollars that should be going into comprehensive universal health care, truly supporting Leave No Child Behind, truly supporting

moderate and low-income housing, truly being used to rebuild the infrastructure that's falling apart all over America.

Come on, Mr. President, don't challenge us this way. There are some of us who know what we're going to do, and others are going to get wise very soon.

PRESIDENT BARACK OBAMA

In 2008, the congresswoman's last-minute support of then candidate Obama helped win the sleek senator from Chicago the Democratic nomination for president. But by 2011, still embroiled in her overdrawn ethics scandal, which had strained some of the congresswoman's political muscle, Waters and Obama weren't exactly on the best of terms. The two were never super tight, according to aides. The generational gap (civil rights era versus multi-culti hope and change), cultural differences (South Central L.A. versus Hawaii), and divergent political philosophies (political machine versus no new friends) all added to their very cool "nice to see you" interactions.

But in 2011, with black unemployment at a record high of 16 percent, Waters, for whom the issue of employment has always been central to her constituency, was ready to rock the boat a bit. That summer, the Congressional Black Caucus (CBC) held town hall meetings on jobs in African American communities hardest hit by the 2008 financial crisis. In Detroit, Waters and her colleagues were catching heat from the gathered crowd on the lack of jobs. The audience wanted to know what, if anything, Congress and the White House were doing about employment. Up to that point, the CBC and the president hadn't sat down to discuss the issue, and in fact, at the time, Obama, campaigning for

president, was on his own economic tour. But his stops were in rural white America. Yet another sticking point. Waters didn't hold back one inch in her response.

"We don't put pressure on the president because y'all love the president. You love the president. When you tell us it's all right and you unleash us, and you tell us you're ready for us to have this conversation, we're ready to have the conversation. . . . All I'm saying to you is, we're politicians. We're elected officials. We are trying to do the right thing and the best thing. When you let us know it is time to let go, we'll let go," said Waters. A frustrated attendee yelled, "Let go!" from the audience. Longtime Michigan congressman John Conyers, who was also at the town hall, agreed. "We should be in front, three to five, six thousand people the day before we open our fortieth conference on Tuesday, September the 20th, in front of the White House, demanding jobs."

The CBC's Annual Legislative Conference, a weeklong Washington event centered on the policy needs of the African American community, was just over a month away. President Obama was scheduled to deliver the keynote speech at the conference's splashy Phoenix Awards gala dinner. Tensions were rising and the ball gowns hadn't even come out of the closet yet.

Two days after the Detroit town hall, Waters, who had clearly gotten the message that it was time to tap on the president's shoulder, went on CNN to ever so politely let Obama know that the streets was talking. "We love the president," the congresswoman told CNN. "We're working with him but are sounding the alarm." She added, "We want the president to know that he's got a lot of people behind him. We're hurting, and we're getting angry. . . . Let the president know that we want him to be tough."

Well, Obama *was* tough.

At the CBC's closing gala that year, the president took the stage and had some straight talk for the folks in the room. After touching on the heartbreak and frustration he knew unemployed black Americans felt, the president closed with a call to action that ruffled a few feathers:

> *So I don't know about you, CBC, but the future rewards those who press on. With patient and firm determination, I am going to press on for jobs. I'm going to press on for equality. I'm going to press on for the sake of our children. I'm going to press on for the sake of all those families who are struggling right now. I don't have time to feel sorry for myself. I don't have time to complain. I am going to press on.*
>
> *I expect all of you to march with me and press on. Take off your bedroom slippers, put on your marching shoes. Shake it off. Stop complaining, stop grumbling, stop crying. We are going to press on. We've got work to do, CBC.*
>
> *God bless you, and God bless the United States of America.*

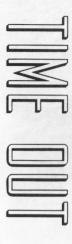

Welp. That did *not* go over well with some folks in the room. The following Monday, *the* Maxine Waters responded with no less than five TV hits. On CBS's *Early Show* the gentle lady from California clapped back with this: "I don't know who he was talking to." Later she told CNN, "Many of those people in the room are civil rights people who have marched, who have worked. We don't have bedroom slippers. We've been out there for years doing this kind of thing." That afternoon on MSNBC she had even more to say. "But I certainly don't believe that he thinks that the Congressional Black Caucus is sitting around in house slippers or bed slippers or whatever the things are. I don't own them and I don't understand the image being described there." My God, the shade. And even as the seventy-three-year-old chided the president she threw him a bone in that same interview, "I don't think he really meant that, and we're not going to hold it against him." Despite winning the 2012 presidential election with a record number of black voters, Obama and Waters's relationship never truly got off the ground after their 2011 disagreements.

CHAPTER SIX

SHUT UP

1992–1994

IN WHICH A TENSE MOMENT IN THIS NARRATIVE
AND ON THE FLOOR OF CONGRESS BECOMES
A DEFINING MOMENT IN A LEADER'S CAREER

The best kind of drama is the kind that you have to dig up a history book and a moldy copy of *Robert's Rules of Order* to understand, and that's exactly what the tale of the Mace is. It involves a symbolic (possibly magical) silver-and-ebony pole, the Whitewater scandal, and more gavel-banging than a season of *Judge Judy*. More important, the tale of the Mace is a quintessential part of Maxine Waters lore, an incident during which her singular understanding of her duties and place in American politics proved to be more than a worthy match for opponents who tried and failed to silence her. So, strap on your bifocals and brush up on your parliamentary procedure; we're going reading.

As you read much of the following recap of a congressional floor brouhaha incited by an investigation into possible impropriety related to a presidential family's real estate investments, you will frequently have the thought, "Well, this is ironic." Trust us, we know. But bear in mind that you are reading this in the present, when almost everything in the political realm is sadly ironic and no one talks about that irony anymore. Don't worry, we will talk about it. In a minute. But first: the past.

It's July 28, 1994. An ascendant Maxine Waters is nearing the end of her first term as the congressperson representing California's 35th District and the midterm elections are looming on the horizon. In three months, the Republican Party will assume control of the House for the first time in forty years, gaining fifty-four seats (but not Maxine Waters's; never Maxine Waters's). In two months, the party will introduce the Contract with America, a set of policy proposals and governmental reforms

Waters in 1994.

RECLAIMING HER TIME

authored by Newt Gingrich and Dick Armey and largely influenced by the conservative think tank the Heritage Foundation. The stated goals: shrinking the size of government and reducing corruption in Congress. ("That's ironic," you mutter, in the future.) The not-so-secondary goal of the Contract, however, will be to make the midterms an issue of national concern, using the Clinton presidency as the antagonist in a narrative about putting the government back to work for the people. Or some such.

On July 28, 1994, all of this—the Contract, the flip, the sea change that would eventually lead to the impeachment of Bill Clinton, the ascension of Newt Gingrich, and Donald Trump's "Drain the Swamp" slogan, the mutated epitome of irony—is bubbling beneath the surface of a congressional hearing.

The House Banking Committee was in its second day of hearing testimony from various members of the Clinton White House pertaining to whether Bill and Hillary Clinton tried to curtail a special counsel investigation into a failed real estate venture, the Whitewater Development Corporation, in which they'd invested in 1979. The Whitewater scandal followed the Clintons from the 1992 campaign trail all the way to the White House, with allegations of everything from financial impropriety to bribery to having certain people bumped off. They were never charged with any crimes, but that didn't stop their Republican opponents from looking for evidence by shaking every branch of every tree that the Clintons had ever planted, sat under, or gazed at fondly. Which is how Maggie Williams, then chief of staff for Hillary Clinton, ended up in front of the House Banking Committee, on which Waters and Republican congressman Peter King served.

Okay, the first thing you need to know is that Whitewater was a big, sprawling mess that could, and has, taken over entire books. But not this one, dear. Suffice it to say, by the time of the July hearings, most Democrats, including Maxine Waters, were publicly very over the investigation and the allegations that the Clintons were trying to exert their influence to curtail the special counsel's work. So, this hearing, like many future hearings relating to presidential impropriety, was split along party lines. While most Democrats used their allotted time to express their bewilderment that the hearing was even taking place, the Republicans on the committee largely ceded their time to a few former prosecutors among their ranks, one of them being Peter King, a curly-haired, bespectacled representative from New York with a sort of Danny Houston vibe.

King latched on to a letter given by former deputy Treasury secretary Roger Altman to Maggie Williams, who then reportedly turned it over to her boss, Hillary Clinton. Altman had given conflicting testimony about his role in Whitewater, but it was alleged that he had tipped the Clintons off to a criminal referral made against them in the Whitewater case through various channels, including the sealed letter. Peter King didn't believe Maggie Williams when she said that she didn't open the letter; Maggie Williams didn't care what King believed. King said that if he received a sealed letter like that, he'd be curious what was in it. Williams, with a deadpan delivery that should have made her a Thursday night Must See TV star, replied, "Sir, my curiosity may not be on par with yours." This exchange went on for five whole American taxpayer–funded minutes.

Where, you say, was Maxine Waters in all of this? That's a good question. She was behind and to the right of King, looking down over his shoulder, like a goddess on Mount Olympus surveying humanity, in which she was not too pleased. In the C-SPAN video of the exchange, you cannot see her as the shot pivots from Williams to King and back again. But you can feel her mounting annoyance radiating in from just off-screen.

After casting aspersions on Williams's claims, King decided to just go for it and accused her of lying to the committee. "I don't believe you," he said. Williams, unflappable, replied, "My honesty in this matter does not depend upon whether or not you believe me." If ever there were a perfect tee-up for Maxine Waters's distinctive brand of truth-telling and nonsense-stopping, it's Maggie Williams's laconic delivery and utter refusal to get caught up in the histrionics. King responded to Williams's retort, but by this time committee chairman Henry B. Gonzalez was already gaveling. King pointed out that he still had time left, and the chairman cut in, telling King that he was gaveling because King was badgering the witness. And here's where it really gets good.

King refuted Gonzalez's assessment, continuing to talk. Maxine Waters chilled at her station above. Gonzalez started to talk over King talking over Gonzalez. Maxine Waters bided her time. Gonzalez started to bang his gavel with more seriousness. And, finally, from Olympus itself, Maxine Waters's voice rose above the fray. "Mr. Chairman, please," she said into the microphone. "The gentleman is out of order."

First of all, you have to love that she chose this moment to interject. You can almost hear the thought, "Okay, I've had enough of this," bubbling to the surface. Second of all, when Maxine Waters tells you "you're out of order," most of us would very quickly find a way to get ourselves in order—our speech, our bodies, our spirits. Put it all in order. King had a different reaction.

"I don't think Ms. Waters has anything to do with this line of questioning," he said over Gonzalez's gavel and Waters's objection. "You had your chance. Why don't you just sit there?"

Oh, yes, he did. He asked Maxine Waters "Why don't you just sit there?" which is definitely a thing that you do not say to Maxine Waters. She will sit, stand, speak, cartwheel, or do magic tricks wherever she pleases.

"You are out of order," she fired back.

"You are always out of order," he replied.

"You're out of order. Shut up!"

And so it begins!

"What was that? What was that last remark?" King asked, whipping around like an incredulous cast member on a *Real Housewives* reunion. "I would like you to say it again." Hon, you heard what she said. Maxine Waters always says what she says, and if you need to revisit the transcript to refresh your memory, that's fine. But she doesn't need to be out here repeating herself. "You heard what I said," she told King. Even though in the C-SPAN footage Waters is still not on camera, the lean she puts into the word "heard" is so strong that it comes sailing out of the screen like you've got 3-D glasses on.

King went back to attempting to question Williams, but Gonzalez was having none of it, reminding King that he was out of order. So, out of order and out of options, King decided to throw one last jab at Waters: "Nobody cares about you," he said, giving it playground-taunt realness.

And that was just day one.

The next day, King came out swinging: "Speaker, last night the Democratic majority on the Banking Committee demonstrated conclusively to the American people how desperate they are to keep the American people from the truth about Whitewater." Wow. Already we're at the precipice of full-blown conspiracy. This is so much. King continued: "Chairman Gonzalez attempted to gag me, and Maxine Waters, the congresswoman from California, interrupted me and told me to shut up. . . . I want her to know that as long as I'm on that committee, as long as I'm in this House, she's not going to tell me to shut up, she's not going to tell the American people to shut up!" In some ways, this plays like the dramatic speech from the end of a John Grisham movie. And maybe that's how it felt. King took the stance that he was being unfairly silenced by Gonzalez and Waters and later asked the rhetorical question of what this situation would be like were it reversed and he had told Waters to shut up.

Now, we don't need to unpack this, as we live in the future and we know that this is an apples-and-oranges comparison. And also, before and after the "shut up" heard round the chamber, King told Waters "you're always out of order" and "nobody cares about you." But "shut up" was the worst thing that happened in their exchange and tantamount to persecution. Okay.

There's also the issue here of a white male congressman repeatedly telling one black woman, Maggie Williams, that she is lying and telling another black woman, Maxine Waters, "nobody cares about you." This interaction, specifically, is not just about partisan politics or decorum; it's not about the order or the lack thereof. It's about respect. Was Peter King disrespecting Williams and Waters? Did his tone, purposely or accidentally, shift from prosecutorial aggressiveness to a more sinister kind of dominance, steeped in white male privilege? And did it matter if that wasn't his intent? This was a moment when Maxine Waters stood up for herself and for another black woman, a moment in which she said the quiet part out loud. This stance was not new for Maxine Waters, nor would it be the last such moment for her. This was the congresswoman being herself, fully—an elected leader who would not tolerate disrespect and would speak truth to power, regardless of the circumstance.

After being recognized by Chairwoman Carrie Meek, Waters strode to the podium in a black suit with wide red lapels and cuffs. There was no trepidation in her face, but also no cockiness; if anything, she looked relaxed: another day at the office. "[King] had to be gaveled out of order," she began, "because he badgered a woman who was a witness from the White House. I'm pleased I was able to come to her defense. Madam Chairwoman, the day is over when men can badger and intimidate women, marginalize them, and keep them from speaking." At this, an unseen male representative cuts in, voicing a complaint and asking that Waters's comments be stricken from the record. A man attempting to erase a woman's speech about women being kept from speaking is rather, what's the word . . . ironic, isn't it? Maxine Waters was undeterred. "We are members of this House! We will not allow men to intimidate us."

Here things get slightly chaotic. Meek started banging her gavel and saying, "Will the gentlewoman suspend," effectively asking Waters to stop speaking. The man's voice continued unabated. And Maxine Waters spoke on. Eventually male members of the House started calling for Waters to be handed the Mace to get her to stop speaking.

The Mace.

Compared to Whitewater, the Mace is actually fairly easy to understand: it's a big fancy pole with a Golden Snitch on top that has magical powers over every member of Congress. See? Easy. In reality, the Mace compromises thirteen ebony poles, representing the original colonies, bound by silver strands and topped by a silver globe and an eagle. The Mace is always present when the House is in session, and though its purpose is largely symbolic, the Speaker of the House can order the sergeant at arms to present the Mace to a member of the

House who is out of order as a disciplinary measure. The idea is that once presented with the Mace, the out-of-order member will return to order. It's like a reverse conch from *Lord of the Flies,* and honestly, don't you wish you had this in everyday life? Someone is out of pocket and you just hand them a magic staff and they get themselves together? You need to order yourself a Mace from Amazon immediately.

The presentation of the Mace almost never happens, one, because most congressional kerfuffles are resolved with conversation and banging of gavels. And two, probably because presenting a ceremonial staff to a person who is really jazzed up may or may not actually make them calm down. So, you may want to put a hold on that Amazon order.

When Representative Peter King got up to speak on the House floor on the morning of July 29, he probably was not intending to get the Mace presented to anyone, even Representative Waters. Perhaps he wanted her reprimanded or censured. Perhaps he just wanted to air a grievance. But the Mace had not been used to discipline a member of Congress in his lifetime, not since World War I, so it's fair to say that this wasn't top of mind. So, it's all the more remarkable that after thirty seconds of a black woman making a declaration of her worth and the worth of her words, suddenly someone was calling for the silence stick to come out of storage.

The *New York Times,* in its report on the matter, would say she spoke angrily, but the video tells a different story. She isn't raising her voice like King was, she isn't banging on the podium—she is speaking clearly, passionately, and strongly about her refusal to be undermined. And maybe to some, coming from a black woman, that sounds like anger. But that's probably because some people haven't been listening right, or at all. Meanwhile, the man's voice continues to rise, from annoyance to frustration to, yes, anger. He begins calling for the sergeant at arms, he wants the House to adjourn. "Madam Speaker, put the question," he screams, imploring the use of the Mace.

"Madam Speaker," Maxine Waters concludes, "this is a fine example of what they try to do to us."

Waters would later say that over the tumult, she was not aware that Meek was asking her to suspend her speech. She had the floor, so she assumed that Meek was asking the man interrupting Waters to stop speaking. Later, Speaker of the House Thomas Foley would announce to the House that in his opinion, though "the words were not in themselves unparliamentary, the chair believes that the demeanor of the gentlewoman was not in good order." Foley ordered that Waters did not have to leave the House but that she could not participate in House business for the rest of the day. He struck her words from the record. But not from history; on this and on many other matters that straddle the line between microaggression and outright disrespect, Maxine Waters would not, and will not, be silenced.

ON DEMEANOR

Let's talk about demeanor for a minute.

For years, nay, for her entire career, Maxine Waters has crossed paths with politicians, usually men, who did not know what to make of her, let's say, demeanor. Is there anything particularly odd about a politician who speaks their mind, forcefully and with great passion? Alexander Hamilton would say, "Hell no!" But there's something specific that ruffles and rankles men on both sides of the aisle. The blowup with Peter King may have been the result of a strange collision between partisan politics and parliamentary procedure (and some good, old-fashioned rudeness), but the scandalized reaction was nothing new for Waters.

What is the core of Maxine Waters's demeanor? Yes, she's forthright and commanding, but she's also funny and sly. There's a kernel of wit embedded even in her fiery retorts to Peter King. Perhaps that's part of it: when faced with opposition, she's not melting down or freaking out. She's not flying off the handle. She's telling you, in no uncertain terms, what she thinks, and if you have a problem with that, well, maybe that's on you, my dude. "People are not accustomed to a woman, in particular an African American woman, taking this kind of leadership," she told CNN's Chris Cuomo in 2017 in reference to another public sparring match, this one with President Donald Trump. The host looked shocked and asked another question about demeanor; the congresswoman had the placid expression of someone for whom neither the question nor the answer was anything new.

Thirty years earlier, in 1987, while trying—and eventually succeeding—to push through an affirmative action amendment on a spending bill in the California Assembly, she'd run afoul of Republican and Democratic assemblymen who opposed affirmative ac-

"PEOPLE ARE NOT ACCUSTOMED TO A WOMAN, IN PARTICULAR AN AFRICAN AMERICAN WOMAN, TAKING THIS KIND OF LEADERSHIP."

tion. Waters won out, which left some men feeling some kind of way about it. State Senator Alfred Alquist churlishly told the *Los Angeles Times*, "Miss Waters is a very aggressive, domineering person who apparently rules the Assembly with an iron hand. She is very difficult to deal with, but you have to admire her determination in fighting for her own beliefs." He actually said this! On the record! Is it a compliment wrapped in a put-down or an attempted read inside of a praise ravioli? Who can say? What are the faults here?

- "Aggressive," another word for assertive, also known as the quality of leadership.
- "Domineering"; hmm, is this code for "talks when I want to talk"? Perhaps.
- "Rules with an iron hand." This is a glowing job performance review!

The real offense, though, is in the second sentence: she is, according to Alquist, "difficult to deal with." This is the surprising one. How can it be that a legislator who successfully and consistently built coalitions and won support for programs that would benefit the poorest and the most disenfranchised could be hard to deal with? How is it that despite massive opposition, this hard-to-deal-with politico had managed to garner enough support to pass the aforementioned affirmative action amendment? If this then-forty-nine-year-old black woman was so hard to deal with, how did she make so many deals?

Or was it not so much that Waters was hard to deal with? What if she just wasn't compliant? What if she just didn't shut up when someone in the halls of power said "shut up"? What if instead of shutting up, she was demanding to be heard and to be engaged with? What if that was the "difficulty"? "I am sick and tired of nice black

Waters in February 1991.

people," Waters once told a crowd at a Los Angeles hearing about, of all things, construction contracts. "Be polite but speak your mind. Get angry and let these people know it. You do have the power."

When told about Alquist's comments, Maxine Waters had the same chill response she would have thirty years later when talking to Chris Cuomo, and the countless times she would be challenged with the false flag of demeanor in between. "Those who consider themselves very important and very powerful," she said, "don't like to be in a position where people who should not be powerful and important are forcing them to respond to them." Hear that!

"WHEN YOU HAVE PEOPLE WHO ARE WILLING TO CHALLENGE THE ESTABLISHMENT, IT'S REALLY DANGEROUS TO THE ESTABLISHMENT."

M.W.

CHAPTER SEVEN

WALL STREET AND GANGSTERS

1992–1994

IN WHICH THE CONGRESSWOMAN STANDS UP
FOR RAP ARTISTS AND GOES AFTER THE BIG BANKS—
ALL AT THE SAME TIME

Here's what you need to know: 2Pac is Maxine Waters's favorite rapper. How many U.S. representatives, offhand, can tell you their favorite rap artist? How many can back it up with a favorite track and verse? How many elected leaders, when asked the question, would answer something like, "Alexander Hamilton in *Hamilton* is my favorite rapper," which, while an acceptable take (no shade here for Lin-Manuel Miranda's Pulitzer Prize–winning explosion of American history), does not actually complete the assignment as given. Looking out on the sea of faces in the floor of the House, you know, in your heart, that far too few would be able to answer the simple question about an American art form, a paradigm shifter, a tool of liberation. Maybe it doesn't matter?

Okay, but let's think about how many preferences and allegiances to other pop culture hallmarks are hammered out and market-researched by politicians and their staffs. Think about how important it is that a politician have a favorite team to root for or a favorite beer. After all, how can someone pass the beer test of electability—that is, whether you'd want to have a beer with this person—if they don't even have a favorite beer? For better or worse, we want our politicians to have trivial predilections and we want those predilections to match our own. We want our representatives to have good taste. In an ideal world, we want to pull a lever in a voting booth for someone who seems to us to be "a real one." Maxine Waters, certified real one, can tell you her favorite rapper and she's been able to do so for years. While many more representatives may also lay claim to being real ones today, in 1994, the congressional class picture and the cultural understanding of rap were much different, and Waters had to be real basically all by herself.

In 1994, the country was in the middle of a conversation about family values and no one could seem to agree on what that meant. Of particular focus was the music industry, which then Second Lady

Tipper Gore had already been taking on the previous decade in her role as a cofounder of the Parents Music Resource Center (PMRC), the committee that was instrumental in getting parental advisory labels placed on albums with content it deemed explicit. While the PMRC set its sights on music of many genres (Cyndi Lauper even got slapped on the wrist for the euphemism-heavy hit "She Bop," which the PMRC rated as "Profane or sexually explicit"), by the mid-1990s there was a particular focus from all angles on a relatively new sound coming out of some of the neighborhoods in Maxine Waters's district: gangsta rap. Noted and beloved for its unfiltered depictions of some realities of black life under economic and state oppression, gangsta rap lyrics often valorized violence, drug use, and gang lifestyles while also capturing the effects of generational poverty, racism, and police brutality. What had started out as an underground art form originated by Philadelphia's Schoolly D had spread to the West Coast and was starting to gain traction in a larger market as artists like Ice-T and Sister Souljah and N.W.A. and, later, 2Pac (Tupac Shakur) got record deals.

Hand-wringing about gang culture in South Central had carried over from the Bush administration to the Clinton administration, but the connection that Waters was making between the total lack of opportunities for the people in her district, particularly young black men, and the rise of gangs as an alternative remained largely unaddressed. However, when those young black men started making record label money, suddenly it was a national crisis. "Don't these politicians realize the country was founded on the kind of revolutionary political thought expressed in my song?" Ice-T told the *Los Angeles Times* in 1992. "I mean, haven't they ever listened to the national anthem? Anybody knows that the 'Star-Spangled Banner' is really just a song about a shoot-out between us and the police." Sister Souljah, an activist, recording artist, and author, said,

The reason why rap is under attack is because it exposes all the contradictions of American culture. What started out as an underground art form has become a vehicle to expose a lot of critical issues that are not usually discussed in American politics. The problem here is that the White House and wannabes like Bill Clinton represent a political system that never intends to deal with inner city urban chaos.

Ice-T's 1992 song "Cop Killer," about a victim of police brutality who seeks vengeance, became a particular flash point of the debate. But the conversation wasn't centered on the ethics of the song, or the specific callouts of Rodney King and Los Angeles police chief Daryl Gates in the lyrics. Instead, it became a straw man for a larger debate about control of creative expression. Boycotts of Ice-T's label, Time Warner, were organized, and eventually the company and gangsta rap would become the subject of hearings in both the House and the Senate in 1995. By this time, rap music had become a $900 million a year industry and showed no signs of peaking. Some of the objections to gangsta rap's content were surely genuine, particularly given the genre's sometimes misogynistic or homophobic lyrics. But Waters had done the thinking around this aspect, too. "While I find some of the language offensive and hard on the ears, I didn't first hear the words whore and bitch from Snoop," she said. "These songs merely mimic and exaggerate what the artists have learned about who we are (as a society). And while it is unacceptable to refer to any person in derogatory terms, I believe rappers are being used as scapegoats here." The fact of the matter was it became a so-called national problem only when the black artists behind it (and the largely white music executives) started making money off it. It all comes down to the financials. Or, to use the words of 2Pac in the song "Gettin' Money": "Damned if I don't, and damned if a ni**a do."

"THE FIRST AND THE FIFTEENTH"

If there was anyone who understood the maddening position these rappers from L.A. found themselves in at this moment, it was Maxine Waters. They were facing the same double standards and systemic injustices that she had been talking about for years, the same ones, she said, that had caused the insurrection. But it seemed that for the first time in her political career she wasn't in a position where she could do something about it.

The 1992 election had returned the White House to Democrats after more than a decade of Republican rule and had also dramatically changed the composition of the House. Well, dramatically, that is, by comparison. The 103rd Congress added 23 women U.S. representatives and 16 minority U.S. representatives to the body. Still, that only meant that in the 435-member House, women increased from 6 percent to 11 percent of the body and people of color increased from 9 percent to 14 percent. The result was that issues that might have previously gotten little attention—say, for instance, women's health or job training programs for minority communities—were increasingly brought to the fore. But it wasn't easy. And there was often intraparty disagreement about what the solutions were. Waters, by this time in her second term, had been surprised by the lack of camaraderie in Congress, as compared to the California Assembly, where, even though she butted heads with colleagues, she enjoyed an esprit de corps. The House was bigger and more impenetrable, and she had to find her own way.

To make matters more complicated, Waters had come to Congress with a reputation for having sharp elbows and an even sharper tongue, and her media ubiquity during the L.A. insurrection had only compounded that fact. She was assigned to the House Banking, Finance, and Urban Affairs Committee, which she considered a punishment. After a check-kiting scandal ensnared 450 members of Congress and was publicized by Minority Whip Newt Gingrich (despite the fact that it involved legislators from both parties), many members of the House were trying to get off the committee and as far away as possible from the words "House" and "banking" in close proximity to avoid the negative association. Waters was, initially, quite the fish out of water on the committee. "Getting on that banking committee and . . . dealing with Wall Street and understanding what a derivative was and being able to deal with hedge funds . . . it's quite different than dealing with the confrontation I used to have with Chief Daryl Gates on the police force here in Los Angeles," she told Angela Rye in an interview years later.

This was a world away from the work she'd done in pounding the pavement of her district, personally teaching job skills classes, and sitting in at the South African consulate. In a 2017 interview on the popular program *The Breakfast Club,* she reflected on this turn in her career:

> *Well, I know that some people say, oh, you're so outspoken, you're confrontational. And I think what happened was this: my career has always been one of challenge and I've always dealt up front with the issues. But for a number of years, my voice was not heard because I'm on the Financial Services Committee and we were dealing with issues that don't get a lot of exposure. . . . People didn't hear me for a long time because I was so concentrated on those issues.*

While that's true—she certainly didn't appear on CNN as regularly as she had a year or two earlier—the move that had been intended to mute her would turn out to be central to her overarching ethos. Because, in the end, it all comes down to money. "Billions is what is spent all the time. But it's not spent on poor people," she told the *Los Angeles Times* in 1993. "Policy, for the most part, has been made by white people in America, not by people of color. And they have tended to take care of those things that they think are important. Whether it's their agricultural subsidies, or other kinds of expenditures that are certainly not expenditures for poor people or for people of color. And so, we have to band together and keep fighting back." Banking, she thought, was the life and death of the country. And access to funds for programs, financial literacy, protection from predatory loans, and jobs were the life and death of the communities that she served. She told *Ebony* in 1992:

> *Whether we're talking about insurance or banking or mortgage interest, they control things. Even things that are strictly supported with tax dollars, such as the Fed Home Loan Board, is headed by a white man with an all-white board of directors. They don't hire blacks for any top positions. And we're talking about taxpayers' money! It's mind-boggling and a real cause for anger. It's also cause for action to make sure that blacks get their fair share. I intend to work on this for the next five years. I'm going to straighten some of these systems out!*

The work would continue far beyond the five years she initially mapped out and it would grow to encompass systems that affect every American and every major financial institution. "These are people who have gotten away with the kind of policies that caused us not to be able to get loans for so many years," she'd declare more than twenty years after first being assigned to the committee. "These are the gangsters on Wall Street. . . . So we are constantly fighting." This task, though it initially seemed so far afield, would not slow down Representative Maxine Waters. She would bring the same fight she always had; she would straighten the systems out for her people. As 2Pac said in "All Eyez on Me," you could depend on her "like the first and the fifteenth."

While Waters chooses a different 2Pac song as her favorite— more on this in a minute—the "All Eyez on Me" lyric has particular resonance when we tell the story of this moment. The first reference point in the phrase "depend on me like the first and the fifteenth" is to the days in the month when public assistance checks come. The word "depend" does a lot of work here—for some living at the margins of society, this form of social support is more than something to expect; it's the difference between eating and not eating, heat and cold, housing and the street. For millions, of all races, the first and the fifteenth are the temporary gateways out of a cycle of poverty and need reinforced by structural inequity.

This cycle is something that the artist knew well, and it's something that Waters knew well, too, having grown up in a single-parent household that often depended on social services. It's a knowledge that she carried with her as she worked to coach others in similar situations through Project BUILD and other initiatives. It's also something with which another representative from California, Lynn Woolsey, was deeply familiar. Woolsey had been one of the twenty-three women who were elected to the House in 1992, and she won her office largely on her track record as a successful businesswoman who had spent three years on public assistance while raising three children. Woolsey, a white woman, proudly claimed the label of "the first former welfare mother to serve in Congress" throughout her career. She was aware, however, that though she certainly had been disenfranchised, she was in a far more privileged position than many others who had had similar experiences. "I was lucky," she said just prior to her election. "I was educated. I could speak English and I was assertive. How does a woman less fortunate than myself get through this?" Though Woolsey's path to leadership certainly hadn't been easy, the way that she was able to shape and reclaim her narrative stands in stark contrast to the opposition that rappers like 2Pac faced when they attempted to reshape theirs.

"The first and the fifteenth" can also be read as a reference to amendments to the Constitution. The Fifteenth Amendment guarantees black people the right to vote for the laws that govern us all and the people who represent our concerns. The First Amendment guarantees, among other things, freedom of expression. And though the conflict over gangsta rap may have started as a means of enacting financial control under the guise of decorum, it boils down to this: a duly elected black woman fighting for the constitutionally guaranteed right to free speech.

"THESE ARE MY CHILDREN"

What Maxine Waters likes best about 2Pac is his sensitivity. While she'd been familiar with him and his work for years, it was the 1994 release of his song "Dear Mama" from the 1995 album *Me Against the World* that opened up an important new side of the artist for her. "[With the release of this song, he] really struck me as somebody who not only was brilliant . . . but had a real sensibility and a heart and an understanding that a lot of people don't have," she told Angela Rye. 2Pac's ode to his mother, Afeni Shakur, takes an unflinching look at their complicated relationship. He raps of his deep commitment to her while also detailing his frustrations with her and with his own failings. The track is a three-dimensional portrait of a family that has struggled against their own vices and against systems that provided no relief. It is, ultimately, a song about the human experiences behind headline-making crises and statistics. "And even as a crack fiend, Mama, you always was a black queen, Mama," 2Pac raps in one of the most famous lines.

This kind of humanity is what Waters always returns to time and again when shaping policy. She is not working with numbers and spreadsheets; she's working with stories and people. As the battle against gangsta rap escalated in Washington, she'd always highlight this aspect of the art form. "I thought it was creative and I thought that it opened up a whole new economic opportunity for black people, where jobs and positions were created, when they wouldn't play rap music on some of the major stations," she said in a 2017 interview. "When you have people who are willing to challenge the establishment, it's really dangerous to the establishment."

Afeni Shakur would express a similar sentiment after her son's death:

> *Creativity, we've always seen as a way for us to survive. We don't like to admit this but, as African Americans in this country—especially those of us who come from this country whose parents and grandparents and great-great-great-grandparents were slaves in this country and now we're still here, with five cents—Tupac taught us so much. Tupac would say to me and my sister, "Y'all stop thinking about that welfare. When you gonna get off of welfare?"*

Drawn to that mix of activism and entrepreneurship, Waters started getting to know 2Pac and other rising rappers, even going so far as to accept their invitation to the annual Mother's Day pro-

> **"THE REASON WHY RAP is under ATTACK is BECAUSE iT EXPOSES ALL THE CONTRADICTIONS OF AMERICAN CULTURE."**

gram that some of them would produce. "Tupac, for me, was very special," she told Angela Rye. The relationship would become more than just that of a politician and an influential constituent; Waters felt a maternal pride for these men who were accomplishing what she hoped for so many men in her district.

A s her relationship with Shakur was developing, Waters also continued to advocate for men who shared his circumstances but not his skills. "Look on a street corner—any street corner —in my congressional district or in any other urban center, and you'll see him. He is a member of our lost generation," she wrote in an editorial in the *Los Angeles Times* announcing a proposed $80 million skills training program aimed at young men.

He is between 17 and 30 years old, the product of a dysfunctional family. Unskilled and without a job, he is living from girlfriend to mother to grandmother. He's not reflected in the unemployment statistics and surely isn't on the tax rolls. If he's driving, it's without a license. If he's bunking in public housing, you won't find his name on the lease. He has a record—misdemeanors if he is lucky, felonies more likely. He was the most visible participant in the Los Angeles uprising, but otherwise he seems almost invisible to society.

The program would be, she said, a crime prevention, birth control, and anti-violence campaign all in one; it would offer counseling, education, and training, and, like Project BUILD, it would offer a stipend, this time one hundred dollars. Once again, for Waters, it was about having a clear understanding of the reality of life for her constituents and then figuring out a clear path to financial improvement. Despite meeting massive GOP opposition, Waters managed to successfully guide her program through negotiations; the funding was reduced to $50 million, but it passed House and Senate votes and was signed into law by Bill Clinton. This was a huge victory for Waters. "The great enemies in our cities are hopelessness and lack of opportunity," she said at the time.

Meanwhile, many others were zeroing in on quite a different enemy in the cities. Public protests against gangsta rap and specific songs began springing up from civic and church groups in New York

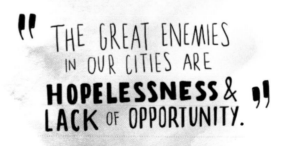

"THE GREAT ENEMIES IN OUR CITIES ARE HOPELESSNESS & LACK OF OPPORTUNITY."

and Los Angeles. Timothy White, then editor in chief of *Billboard,* dismissed it as a particularly pernicious phase: "Rap will likely grow out of the adolescent gullibility of its gangsta pose. Still, it seems only appropriate that any individuals who peddle hatred for profit should earn the greatest censure possible until they either wise up or simply cease and desist."

Dr. bell hooks took issue with the misogyny in many of the songs, comparing it to crack. "It gives [rappers] a sense that they have power over their lives when they don't," she told the *New York Times.* Radio stations began pulling songs from the air due to pressure from politicians and even the chairman of the Federal Communications Commission. Inevitably, Washington got formally involved. In February 1994, the House and the Senate held hearings about the issue of gangsta rap. Maxine Waters was front and center as one of the art form's staunchest defenders. "It would be a foolhardy mistake to single out poets as the cause of America's problems," she said after the House hearings, directly opposing testimony offered from the likes of C. DeLores Tucker, a respected black activist and chairwoman of the National Political Congress of Black Women. "We have declared war against gangsta rap," Tucker told the *Los Angeles Times.* "If the record industry doesn't want to clean itself up, then we'll get the government to step in and help them out. We aim to put a stop to the distribution of these derogatory negative stereotypical images by any means necessary."

The two women faced off again the following week, when both testified in front of the Senate hearing. Also in attendance was the singer Dionne Warwick, who didn't let the fact that she and Waters were friends stop her from delivering a scorching testimony in opposition to Waters's position. Warwick dismissed Snoop Doggy Dogg, another controversial figure at the time, as a "little boy" who "can't even spell ho; he can't spell gangster." Warwick was fired up about the music she described as filth. "I personally am hurt, I am angered," she said. "When will responsibility be demanded by all to deny the continuing images that degrade our dignity, insult our families, stunt the emotions of our children, and most importantly our communities?"

From Waters's perspective, the moral responsibility was not to protect the nation from rap, but to protect these rappers. "These are my children," she testified. "Indeed, they are your children, too. They have invented this art form originally to describe their pains and fears and anger with us as adults." In an echo of her defense of the L.A. insurrection, she asked how anyone expected people to grow up under the conditions that some rappers grew up under and not come away angry. She read lyrics from Snoop Doggy Dogg's song "Murder Was the Case" to show a more profound and pained side of the artist. And she, again, tried to impress upon those gathered that the songs that they found objectionable reflected a reality that was even more objectionable. She would always side with the people over the idea.

"For the past three years, I have brought rap artists to the Congressional Black Caucus' annual legislative weekend. I created this forum because I knew what was coming. I wanted us to get to know them and to interact with them. . . . I do this because I am in the business of transformation," she explained. The congresswoman concluded her remarks by detailing personal relationships she was building with some rappers, including Queen Latifah, who had received a standing ovation from the Black Women's Forum. And she brought the attention back around to the skills program that she had won funding for a year earlier, detailing its success and revealing that she had gotten the financial support of some of gangsta rap's biggest names—Snoop Doggy Dogg, Dr. Dre, Ice Cube, and Ice-T—to financially support five thousand additional young men in the program. Not only was she making sure that these success stories continued to secure the bag, but she was coaching them on how to spread the good fortune. It all comes back to the financials, and from that, freedom.

The hearings did not result in any decisive action for or against gangsta rap and, while rap continued its ascendancy, the moral question became central in the presidential campaign. Bob Dole, a senator who had thrown his hat into the ring for the Republican presidential nomination, gave a tetchy speech at a 1995 fund-raiser in which he decried Hollywood and the music industry for, as he said, undermining our character as a nation. He took particular issue with gangsta rap and Time Warner, which sold the second-most rap albums, including the controversial "Cop Killer." "You have sold your souls, but must you debase our nation and threaten our children as well?" he asked rhetorically. The following day, former secretary of education William J. Bennett delivered a letter to the company's board demanding that Time Warner stop distributing gangsta rap altogether. He was joined, in an unlikely alliance, by C. DeLores Tucker, who also signed the letter. Though Tucker and Bennett were opposed on many other matters, they recognized a common enemy in gangsta rap and targeted Time Warner. "This is not about parties and politics. It is about forestalling America's slide toward decivilization," they wrote in a coauthored *New York Times* opinion piece titled "Lyrics from the Gutter." "There is now a wide consensus that our culture has grown increasingly vulgar, coarse and violent."

N.W.A.'s Ice Cube, in a 1994 dialogue with revolutionary poet Abiodun Oyewole, laid out the disconnect from more established black leadership that he and many other rappers were experiencing: "Some rappers want to put knowledge in their records, and some rappers don't," he said. "You got the older generation of so-called leaders want to come talk to us, want to sit down and rap to us. But it's no dialogue there." The difference between the many leaders who decried rap and Waters was one of respect. "Some people would like to build a wall around the ghetto to keep the rappers quiet," Russell Simmons, founder of Def Jam Records, said in a 1994 interview. "But Maxine understands the conditions that trigger the rage in the music. I've got news for the people who want to shut rap down: It ain't going to happen."

Keeping rap music alive and thriving was, for Waters, a moral imperative, a political act, an act of restorative justice on par with her fight with the banks, her marching in the street, and her skills programs. It was all connected and it was all pushing the culture forward: "Before rap, there was no other platform for talented people like Snoop or Ice Cube or Latifah to speak their minds," she told the *Los Angeles Times*. "These are artists with a message and they're forcing America to listen. It isn't just free speech that we're talking about defending here, it's a social movement. And that's what people can't stand to confront."

"DEAR MAMA"

Maxine Waters continues to host the "Young, Gifted and Black" panel on hip-hop at the Congressional Black Caucus Legislative Conference every year. During the event, leaders bring together established artists like Common, Ra the MC, Rhymefest, and others to share their art and their guidance for emerging artists seeking to make a way for themselves in the business. It acts as both a celebration and a ladder up in an often opaque industry. Waters also maintains her strong ties and allegiances with the rap community and has

T.I. hugs Waters at the Forty-Seventh Annual CBC Legislative Conference.

seen artists like Snoop Dogg, Queen Latifah, Ice-T, and Ice Cube attain worldwide fame and success.

In 2010, the Library of Congress chose 2Pac's "Dear Mama" as the third rap music selection to be included in its National Recording Registry, a collection of recordings deemed "culturally, historically or aesthetically significant." Each year, the Library of Congress chooses twenty-five such songs, albums, radio broadcasts, or podcasts out of thousands of nominations. As of this writing, there are currently nine songs or albums in the National Recording Registry's rap category. Besides "Dear Mama" they include such classics as Jay-Z's *The Blueprint*, *The Miseducation of Lauryn Hill*, Public Enemy's *Fear of a Black Planet*, and *Straight Outta Compton* by N.W.A., the California group that was one of the earliest success stories of gangsta rap and one of its earliest political targets.

The Work

Congressional legislation runs the gamut from resolutions designating awareness days and weeks or expressing sentiments or positions, to bills naming post offices and creating acts. Unless you're glued to C-SPAN, you probably miss a large portion of the legislative business that happens day in and day out. If you watched *Schoolhouse Rock* you know the process by which a bill becomes a law, and that most bills die in committee (dark for a cartoon, when you think about it). So, while the laws that do reach the president's desk can make dramatic differences in the lives of millions of Americans, they only make up a portion of the work of a U.S. representative. Additionally, as you'll see below, you're far more likely to see a given legislator's name as a cosponsor for a bill than as sponsor due to the sheer number of representatives in the House. According to a 2014 study by the Brookings Institution, for instance, in the 114th Congress, the average number of bills introduced per representative was 15.3. So, while these enacted pieces of legislation are the ones that Waters originated, she has cosponsored and helped to shepherd hundreds more into laws.

ENACTED SPONSORED LEGISLATION

BILL NUMBER: H.R. 289

INTRODUCED: January 6, 2005

CONGRESS: 109th

TIMELINE: Passed the House by voice vote on February 1, 2005; passed the Senate by unanimous consent on June 29, 2005; signed into law by President George W. Bush on July 12, 2005

COSPONSORS: 49 cosponsors (33 Democrat, 16 Republican)

PURPOSE: To designate the facility of the U.S. Postal Service located at 8200 South Vermont Avenue in Los Angeles, California, as the "Sergeant First Class John Marshall Post Office Building."

NOTES: Army Sergeant First Class John W. Marshall was struck and killed by a grenade on April 8, 2003, in Baghdad, Iraq. At fifty, he was the oldest soldier in his brigade and one of the soldiers killed in the war in Iraq. He joined the army at eighteen and had served all of his adult life, save for a four-year leave of absence during which he battled Hodgkin's lymphoma.

BILL NUMBER: H.R. 1116

SHORT TITLE: Honest FHA Originator Act of 2009

INTRODUCED: February 23, 2009

CONGRESS: 111th

TIMELINE: See notes.

COSPONSORS: Steve Driehaus (D-OH), Jackie Speier (D-CA)

PURPOSE: To improve the process through which loan originators participate in Federal Housing Administration (FHA) mortgage programs, and for other purposes.

IN OTHER WORDS: This bill and the law that it eventually became a part of are intended to help home owners avoid predatory lending practices by barring lenders with a history of predatory practices from participating in FHA programs.

NOTES: Parts of this bill were incorporated into S. 896–111th Congress: Helping Families Save Their Homes Act of 2009. It was introduced on April 24, 2009;

passed the Senate 91–5 on May 6, 2009; passed the House 367–54 with changes on May 19, 2009; the Senate agreed to the changes on May 19, 2009; signed into law by President Obama on May 20, 2009.

BILL NUMBER: H.R. 4573

SHORT TITLE: Haiti Debt Relief and Earthquake Recovery Act of 2010

INTRODUCED: February 2, 2010

CONGRESS: 111th

TIMELINE: Passed the House by voice vote on March 10, 2010; passed the Senate by unanimous consent with changes on June 30, 2010; House agreed to the changes on April 14, 2010; signed into law by President Obama on April 26, 2010.

COSPONSORS: 69 cosponsors (66 Democrat, 3 Republican)

PURPOSE: To urge the secretary of the Treasury to instruct the U.S. executive directors at the International Monetary Fund, the World Bank, the Inter-American Development Bank, and other multilateral development institutions to use the voice, vote, and influence of the United States to cancel immediately and completely Haiti's debts to such institutions, and for other purposes.

Waters and Representative Barney Frank, former chair of the House Financial Services Committee, make calls in 1998.

NOTES: Waters said, "I authored this legislation because Haiti's immense debt burden would have severely impeded the country's recovery efforts. . . . To help Haiti move forward, I am focused on making sure that durable forms of shelter continue to be delivered and distributed to the millions of survivors living in the camps for the displaced, so that they stay dry and protected from disease during the impending rainy season. Additionally, I will be assisting Haitian small business people and nongovernmental organizations in forming partnerships with the United States Agency for International Development (USAID) so that they have a substantive role in the rebuilding of their country."

BILL NUMBER: H.R. 5569

SHORT TITLE: National Flood Insurance Program Extension Act of 2010

INTRODUCED: June 22, 2010

CONGRESS: 111th

TIMELINE: Passed the House by voice vote on June 23, 2010; passed the Senate by unanimous consent on June 30, 2010; signed into law by President Obama on July 2, 2010.

COSPONSORS: Barney Frank (D-MA), Walter Jones (R-NC), Paul Kanjorski (D-PA), Virginia Brown-Wait (R-FL), Jim Cooper (D-TN), Alcee Hastings (D-FL), Rubén Hinojosa (D-TX)

PURPOSE: To extend the National Flood Insurance Program until September 30, 2010.

NOTES: At the time, Waters said, "This legislation addresses the challenges posed to communities nationwide by the imposition of new flood maps. I saw these challenges in my home city of Los Angeles, and earlier this year, I was able to assist homeowners in the Park Mesa Heights area of Los Angeles who had been mistakenly placed in a flood zone. In this case, FEMA acted quickly to respond to new data and correct the mistake. However, there are thousands of homeowners nationwide who now find themselves in flood zones and subject to mandatory purchase requirements. H.R. 5114 will protect them."

BILL NUMBER: H.R. 3827

SHORT TITLE: Project-Based Voucher Improvement Act of 2015

INTRODUCED: October 23, 2015

CONGRESS: 114th

TIMELINE: See notes.

COSPONSORS: N/A

PURPOSE: To improve the program under section 8 of the U.S. Housing Act of 1937 for using amounts of rental voucher assistance for project-based rental assistance, and for other purposes.

NOTES: This bill was incorporated into H.R. 3700: Housing Opportunity Through Modernization Act of 2016, which was introduced on October 7, 2015; passed the House on February 2, 2016; passed the Senate on July 14, 2016; signed into law by President Obama on July 29, 2016.

BY THE NUMBERS

TOTAL # OF SPONSORED PIECES OF LEGISLATION: 488

TOTAL # OF COSPONSORED BILLS OR RESOLUTIONS: 3,847

TOTAL # OF BILLS SPONSORED: 318

TOTAL # OF AMENDMENTS SPONSORED: 88

TOTAL # OF RESOLUTIONS SPONSORED: 64

TOTAL # OF SPONSORED BILLS THAT WERE SIGNED INTO LAW: 5

TOTAL # OF COSPONSORED BILLS THAT WERE SIGNED INTO LAW: 256

AVERAGE NUMBER OF PIECES OF LEGISLATION WATERS SPONSORED PER MEETING OF CONGRESS: 33

MOST PIECES OF LEGISLATION WATERS SPONSORED IN A MEETING OF CONGRESS: 48, 115th Congress (2017–18)

FEWEST PIECES OF LEGISLATION WATERS SPONSORED IN A MEETING OF CONGRESS: 15, 103rd Congress (1993–94)

AVERAGE NUMBER OF BILLS OR RESOLUTIONS WATERS COSPONSORED PER CONGRESS: 256

MOST BILLS OR RESOLUTIONS WATERS COSPONSORED IN A MEETING OF CONGRESS: 376, 110th Congress (2007–2008)

FEWEST BILLS OR RESOLUTIONS WATERS COSPONSORED IN A MEETING OF CONGRESS: 134, 104th Congress (1995–96)

TOP FIVE SUBJECT AREAS COVERED BY LEGISLATION SPONSORED BY WATERS: Housing and Community Development (56 bills or resolutions)

Health (51)

Finance and Financial Sector (46)

Crime and Law Enforcement (38)

Internal Affairs (34)

Waters in 1998, during a House Judiciary Committee hearing.

CHAPTER EIGHT

THERE ARE LOWS TO THIS

2008–2011

IN WHICH THE CONGRESSWOMAN FIGHTS
FOR HER LEGACY, LEAVES IT ALL ON THE TABLE,
AND FIREWORKS ENSUE

The word "saga" gets tossed around a lot. Your trip to the Trader Joe's downtown in the middle of rush hour for a case of Two-Buck Chuck? A saga. That one time you accidentally pressed the close-doors button just as your boss was running for the elevator—and your face was the last thing she saw? Saga. The horror of having to figure out your Netflix, Hulu, and Disney+ passwords after buying a new smart TV? *Sah-guh*. Those of us with very little actual drama in our lives live to create it, at least in the retelling. But for Maxine Waters, a woman with legislative battle scars of epic proportions, the fight of her political life was, indeed, a saga.

It all started with a little thing known as the worst financial crisis of a generation. Congress had just returned from the 2008 summer recess. It had been a banner year for the words "hope" and "change," but the country was on the cusp of a second Great Depression. As a senior member of the House Financial Services Committee, Maxine Waters had a front-row seat to the shit storm that was about to go down. She needed to do something. Over the August break, Senator Barack Obama had become the first African American to win their party's nomination for president, at the Democratic National Convention in Denver. Waters, who had originally thrown her significant political weight behind Hillary Clinton, was one of the superdelegates who pushed Obama over the top at the eleventh hour. In short, the woman was busy. It was an exciting and stressful time and Waters wasted none of it. Back in the office on Monday, she got to work.

One of the first orders of business was dialing Treasury secretary Henry Paulson's number. Waters wanted to set up a meeting between Paulson and the National Bankers Association (NBA), a decades-old trade group that represented 103 minority-owned banks. Waters had a years-long relationship with the NBA, speaking at its conferences and advocating for its membership on the Hill.

The association had previously contacted the Treasury Department to try to schedule a meeting on its own but hadn't heard back. The collective membership was worried about the future, so they reached out to Waters as well, asking for her help in getting a face-to-face with the treasurer. The bankers were concerned about the impact the financial crisis would have on their business. Many had invested deeply in Fannie Mae and Freddie Mac, whose stock was plummeting as the mortgage crisis worsened. In her telling, Waters wanted to make sure that small minority-owned banks were heard.

"Why is it that Bank of America, Wells Fargo, and Chase Manhattan can get on the telephone and get the treasurer on the phone, can walk in. Why do they have such access?" Waters would ask at a press conference detailing her actions more than two years later. She called Paulson and told the secretary that she had "some people in town who were important to her" and they needed a sit-down. He agreed.

"The system has not adequately recognized that it is not open and available to everybody," Waters would later explain. "I, as an African American woman, must be aware of what I can do to open up the system to everybody and really this is what it's all about." As she saw it, this was Waters's job—giving the marginalized and overlooked a seat at the table. What followed, however, was far from a pat on the back. For her trouble, Maxine Waters was investigated by the House Ethics Committee and formally charged with violating House conflict of interest rules. Strap in, things are about to get real Washington.

So, a day after being contacted by Waters, Paulson took the meeting with the National Bankers Association. Things went, well, weird. At the meeting, which the congresswoman did not attend, two executives dominated the room—Kevin Cohee and Robert Cooper. The men were there representing the NBA but were also senior executives at OneUnited Bank. During the meeting, they made point-blank appeals not just for the one hundred banks of the association but specifically for their own institution. They wanted to know if OneUnited would get back the $50 million in capital it had invested in Fannie Mae and Freddie Mac, which was all but wiped out after the federal government took over the mortgage lenders. Maybe there was a novelty check in the back somewhere? There wasn't. The request wasn't just tacky, it was highly problematic. Thing was, Waters's husband, Sidney Williams, had previously served on the board of OneUnited and at the time held 3,500 shares in the bank, which at their height were worth about $350,000. This was awkward.

After that initial sit-down with the Treasury Department, OneUnited would eventually receive federal bailout money under TARP—the Troubled Assets Relief Program, created to stabilize the economy. Under TARP, signed into law in October 2008, weeks after the meeting Waters arranged between the NBA and Paulson, OneUnited received $12 million. Once Waters learned that Cooper and Cohee were interested in securing TARP funds for OneUnited and were not solely advocating for the NBA as a whole, she knew

"THE SYSTEM HAS NOT ADEQUATELY RECOGNIZED THAT IT IS NOT OPEN & AVAILABLE TO EVERYBODY."

she was in a pickle. *My name is Bennett and I ain't in it.* She even approached her friend Barney Frank, then the chair of the Financial Services Committee, about the conflict due to her husband's shares. Frank advised Waters to "stay out of it" and informed the congresswoman that his office would take over. OneUnited had headquarters in Massachusetts, Barney's turf, so Frank's office wrote a provision in the bailout legislation to help the only African American–owned bank in his home state. He told the *Wall Street Journal* that Waters's interest "had zero impact on the outcome because I would have done it anyway."

Are you still with us? Have you completely wonked out? Basically, the calls and meetings and the millions looked shady AF, as if Waters were trying to line her own pockets by pulling the levers of the political machine. The whole thing smelled like swamp, an example of Washington at its worse. Perhaps it was the very same kind of corruption that originally prompted Waters to enter public office some thirty years before.

Major newspapers sniffed out the story. Articles began popping up in the *Wall Street Journal,* the *New York Times,* and the *Washington Post* connecting Waters to OneUnited and the $12 million in TARP funds. A target was drawn on Waters's back and soon the House Ethics Committee took aim. In early August 2010, nearly two years after Waters made that call to Paulson, the Ethics Committee released an investigative report alleging that Waters had violated conflict of interest rules by picking up that phone. The mud was thrown, and Maxine wasn't in the mood.

To say her reputation was at stake would be an epic understatement. Waters was in line to take over the chairmanship of the House Financial Services Committee when Frank retired. The ethics investigation would not only paint a hideous scarlet asterisk over her decades of public service; it would halt her reach for the gavel. The congresswoman had no choice but to fight it, not that she would have done anything else because, come on, this is Maxine Waters we're talking about.

She refused to settle with the committee by admitting some form of guilt behind the scenes and accepting an official reprimand, which is what most members did in order to avoid a drawn-out process. Also, 2010 was a campaign year. But nah. Nobody puts Mad Max in a corner. "I won't go behind closed doors. I won't cut a deal," she said. Waters wanted her day in "court," so instead of copping to even an iota of wrongdoing, Waters held a press conference on August 13, 2010, two days before she was to turn seventy-two. Happy birthday; here's a room filled with journalists who've been questioning your integrity for months. And in true Maxine fashion it was glorious.

The press conference itself was completely unprecedented. The subjects of ethics investigations don't normal seek out the spotlight. But Waters wanted the media to get its facts straight. Like literally at one point she told the gathered reporters they weren't doing their jobs right. She even told the photographers crouched too close to her podium that they needed to fall back. "You're distracting me . . . And when your lights go off it bothers my eyes." The woman was reading folks who were there to cover the presser *she* called!

"I want to be absolutely clear about one thing," Waters declared. "This case is not just about me. This case is about access. It's about access for those who are not heard by the decision makers." She gathered steam. "The question should not be why I called Secretary Paulson, but why I *had* to. Why a trade association representing 100 banks could not get a meeting at the height of the crisis." She was on a roll. "I admit there are some who do not believe in my philosophy or my methods, but no one should question my devotion to public service."

"In sum," she said in plain English for the cheap seats, "no benefit. No improper action. No failure to disclose. No one influenced. No case."

You would be forgiven for thinking the mic dropped there. It didn't. Next up was a thirty-minute PowerPoint presentation by Mikael Moore, Maxine's grandson and chief of staff. A graduate of Morehouse College, the thirty-two-year-old had spent months trying to convince his grandmother, whom he only referred to as "Congresswoman" while on the Hill, that he'd make a good chief of staff. Waters hadn't had a number one in years but eventually, in 2007, Moore got the top gig. Now, just a few years in, Moore was fighting for his reputation, and the congresswoman's and the family's legacy. No wonder he'd bought a bike to take long rides through Capitol Hill to relieve stress. But Moore wasn't sweating once he got the mic that Friday at the presser. He calmly ran through slide to slide, displaying emails, statements, and other key documents that, according to Waters's office, proved the congresswoman was simply doing her job when she connected the National Bankers Association to the Treasury Department.

"This is what I do," she told reporters later. "This is what I consider as part of my responsibility as a legislator, as a member of Congress." After about an hour and ten minutes, Waters and her staff walked out of the room having laid out their facts in the court of public opinion. The hope was that the ethics trial would begin the following month, in which the committee's staff of lawyers would act as prosecutors and members of the jury. The entire process should've been wrapped up by the fall, optimistically before the November 2010 election. But when do sagas follow commonsense timelines? Things got messy, honey.

The House Ethics Committee had its own issues. That September the committee's staff director sent a memo to the committee's chair alleging that two investigators under the director's supervision had secretly leaked information regarding Waters's case to Republicans on the committee. *Drama!* Already there had been Tyler Perry-level partisan infighting, with Republicans accusing Democrats of going too easy on one of their own. Eventually the staff director and the two staffers he called out left the committee. The case, still unresolved, was put on hold.

In August 2011, the House shelled out more than $500,000 to hire Washington lawyer Billy Martin, who once represented Monica Lewinsky, to investigate whether the House Ethics Committee *could* investigate Waters. After Martin determined the committee hadn't screwed things so badly that it would have to drop its charges against Waters, the lawyer was then put in charge of the investigation himself. Because clearly Ethics did not, in fact, have its own *ish* together.

Another year would go by before Waters was eventually cleared of all charges. In September 2012, the Ethics Committee announced its unanimous decision to drop all charges against the powerful California Democrat. The congresswoman hadn't violated any House rules. The ten-member panel, divided evenly between Democrats and Republicans, did, however, serve an admonishment to Moore, Waters's grandson and chief of staff. Moore was issued "a letter of reproval" by the committee, which said the staffer should have known of Waters's ties to OneUnited and, as Waters directed, should have stopped working on behalf of the

Waters confers with a staff member in 2011.

bank. The letter of reproval is the lightest sanction the committee can hand down, like a tap on the shoulder.

It was a win, but it was hard fought and the battle took its toll on Waters. When the news broke that Waters would be exonerated, there wasn't a ticker tape parade. Waters didn't hold a press conference. Her office didn't even respond to requests for comment or release an official statement of its own. She was seventy-four.

"On any normal day, she is a hard-charging, outspoken, prominent black female legislator," Sean Bartlett, who served as Waters's communications director for the entirety of the ethics investigation, told Helena in an interview. "Layer on top of all that the fight of her life to defend a record of forty years of fighting for the underdog and having that misconstrued and truly vilified in certain corners of Washington . . . that weighed on her. There's no doubt that that affected her."

After decades in the ring, Waters had to be tired. Sure, she scored a "W," but at what cost? The times? They were a-changing. Her constituents stood by her throughout the investigation, electing her to her twelfth term in 2012. But the 43rd District was looking less like it did when she first came to Washington. The Ethics Committee's ruling cleared her path to one day running the House Financial Services Committee, but was she ready to climb that Hill?

No career is constantly on the upswing; there are lows. What's particularly striking about Waters's tough years is that she never stopped being the outspoken advocate she's always been. In the midst of both her ethics investigation and her needling the White House, the congresswoman repeated five words: "This is what I do," she told *Politico* in an October 2011 interview about her tendency to speak truth to power no matter the costs. It's what she does. She stays in the game.

CHAPTER NINE

SHE BETTA WERK

IN WHICH THE UNCOMPROMISED STYLE BEHIND ALL THAT SUBSTANCE IS PROPERLY CELEBRATED

Maxine Waters was on fire. It was a steamy Saturday night in August 2017—some nine months after Donald J. Trump had been elected president ("I don't honor him, I don't respect him, and I don't want to be involved with him"), five months after Waters unapologetically called for his impeachment ("He's a liar! He's a cheat! He's a con man. We've got to stop his ass!"), and just one month after schooling Treasury secretary Steve Mnuchin on *Robert's Rules of Order* ("Reclaiming my time")—and Congresswoman Maxine Waters was hot. Burning, in fact.

Decked out from head to toe in all red, Waters sashayed onto the stage of the annual Black Girls Rock! Awards on that summer night like a woman on the verge of a major breakthrough. She was just two weeks shy of her seventy-ninth birthday and was stunting on them in a body-skimming fire-engine knit number that hit just below the knee. The dress showed a little shoulder, gave 'em a little leg, and kept it classy AF. Waters's matching heels were as high as the congresswoman could handle—so stiletto—and she topped the outfit off with her signature red lip. In a word, the septuagenarian was sexy. And the crowd went completely nuts. How many grandmas do *you* know who are out here serving up lewks *and* calls for impeachment? The answer is none. No grandmas. Zero.

"She was so fly and sexy at nearly eighty years old," former *Essence* fashion and beauty editor Michaela Angela Davis recalled in an interview with Helena. Davis was on her feet in the auditorium that night when "Auntie Maxine" arrived to receive the Social Humanitarian Award for, according to BET, "being a fearless and outspoken advocate" for underserved populations. For Davis, that image of the congresswoman dressed to slay solidified why Maxine Waters had become a universal symbol of resistance over that previous year. "I mean she's not trying to disappear for anybody. At eighty she's giving body." That bears repeating. At eighty. She's. Giving. Body. Your Nana could never.

While swathed in the aforementioned red dress and heels, Waters, enjoying her reintroduction to the national zeitgeist as "Auntie Maxine," delivered an equally fiery speech aimed at her haters (the Tea Party, Trump, the mediocre in general) and her congratulators (everybody else).

"I want you to know, if it was not for the love and respect shown to me by black women, those right-wing ultraconservative alt-right haters in this country, they would have me believe I'm too black, I'm too confrontational, I'm too tough, and I'm too disrespectful of them. But now," she said pausing ever so slightly for effect, "I know I'm simply a strong black woman." The glitzy tennis bracelet on Maxine's wrist reflected the light as she underlined those last three words, emphasizing the description "strong black woman" with her right hand, as strong black women are wont to do.

"I am you and you are me," she told the crowd of women, now whipped up in a "yassssssssss, girl" frenzy. "We have power. We have influence. We can do things others have told us we can't do. I don't care how big you are, I don't care how high you are, if you come for me, I'm coming for you," the congresswoman added to thunderous

Waters strikes a pose at 2017's Black Girls Rock!

applause. And she did all that dressed like a walking warning sign, wordlessly telegraphing her message to her fans in the room and her foes outside of it. It was masterful and by no means unintentional.

If you think personal style is trivial, that the clothes one wears have nothing more to say about the individual wearing them than "hey, this was clean," then this chapter isn't for you. But if you've been paying attention, looking closely at the choices women *and* men make every day to signal where they came from, who they are, and what they believe in, then pull up a chair.

Although her millennial moniker "auntie" might call to mind a certain stuffiness wrapped in paisley, that's not the Auntie Maxine the kids are talking about. Waters is formal without being fussy. She is the First Lady of your neighborhood First AME Church of I Did Not Wake Up Like This (It Takes Skill, Little Girl) mixed with your local high school principal who's been at this for thirty years with a pinch of your twice-divorced auntie who told you to never settle for your boring college boyfriend. No, Maxine's auntie is iconic, never archaic. "She is the swaggy, sexy, will-cuss-you-out auntie," said Davis. Think Wynona from *Good Times* with a Neiman Marcus card. Glamorous at eighty-one, Waters hasn't given up on the idea of being both powerful and sexy. She is unquestionably commanding and uniquely feminine, two adjectives too often pitched against each other, especially for African American women. She wears outfits that hug her body instead of hiding it in boxy Capitol Hill–approved suits or sheaths. Her skirts sometimes hit above the knee. She sports colors like electric blue that make her stand out in a crowd. The woman has no interest in fading away in the man-

Waters in stripes in 2019.

ner society expects, shall we say, mature woman to vanish politely. "She amplifies herself," said Davis. "She turns her clothes on."

In a 1989 profile of Waters, *Los Angeles Times* reporter Ronald Brownstein described Maxine, having by then served nearly a dozen years in the California State Assembly, thus: "In this era of smooth, unoffensive, indistinguishable elected officials, Waters is defiantly anomalous, a bantamweight throwing jabs in a room of game-show hosts. There's nothing pastel about Waters; she lives in primary colors." He might have been describing her closet as well. The congresswoman doesn't do pastels. When it comes to Maxine's style, matronly and conservative aren't in her fashion lexicon. She does not shy away from anything—bold colors, baubles, or bare legs.

"She walks through the world as if she doesn't give a fuck about what you think about her," said Davis. "She's not trying to make anyone feel comfortable. I don't think she's ever felt the need to not be authentic. You can feel it in her. She has shown us in her politics that she's not afraid of them and she says what she wants to say. I don't think she would abandon that same notion in her sense of style. I think she thinks about who she is."

Veteran *Wall Street Journal* fashion reporter Teri Agins agrees that Waters's fashion choices are "considered," a word that gives us *Downton Abbey* vibes. It's an old-school approach to fashion in which the outfit speaks in concert with its wearer. Waters is a woman for whom the term "ensemble" applies, with every piece of her outfit considered in concert with one another. "She's very chic. She carries herself like a lady. It's a sophisticated coordination," Agins told Helena in an interview. "She's assertive and the clothes are part of that."

The congresswoman grew into her political power alongside the women's revolution, when fashion designers woke up to the working-woman's needs and began to create looks for the female executive. St. John, Armani, Oscar de la Renta, and Carolina Herrera were the new uniform for the pulled together and powerful. It's the power look, the look of success. But "label chaser" Waters is not. "I think she's more clever than that," said Agins. While the congresswoman always looks expensive, that doesn't mean the clothes she wears necessarily are. This is a woman who loves to vintage shop, who can go into a so-called thrift store and come out looking like a million bucks. "She has a good eye and I think that's all a part of her. Women of that generation knew how to make something out of nothing.

Waters attends the 2019 California Democratic Party State Convention.

They were thrifty, knew how to stretch money and bargain shop. It was called 'cheap chic,' but the word I would use would be 'resourceful,'" Agins added.

Waters knows you're watching when she enters a room, and so she shows up prepared for the attention, the occasion of your admiration. "To me it has this sort of self-awareness that she's going to draw attention because of who she is," explained Robin Givhan, the *Washington Post*'s Pulitzer Prize–winning fashion critic. "And if you're looking her way, she's going to make sure that she's looking her best." Basically, what you won't do is catch Congresswoman Maxine Waters out here looking anything but ready.

Givhan described Waters's look as pulled together. "It's very polished, it's very considered, it's accessorized. She's not just throwing on a suit in the morning, she's getting dressed. She is *dressing*."

Dressing is a lost art that is deeply rooted in the optics of political protests for children of the civil rights era. And here you thought Maxine was just throwing the doors of her walk-in closet open and choosing a blazer at random. In the 1950s and '60s "how you dressed," said Givhan, "was directly related to your sense of self-respect." Black folks raised in the middle of the last century did not simply wear clothes. "You were dressing as a matter of your own dignity," Givhan went on. "You were going out into the world as a representative of your people." And here's the thing—that's not fair. But, in Maxine's own words when recalling her time working in a segregated restaurant, that's just how it was.

The hypervisibility and vigilance that came with looking the part all the time, Givhan said, "is foreign to someone who is of this era." Gen Xers and millennials raised on *Free to Be . . . You and Me* can't truly relate to the immense effort their grandmothers and grandfathers put into their everyday battle attire—suits, ties, pantyhose, and gloves were armor in and of themselves. For Maxine's generation, getting dressed was as political an act as plopping down at a lunch counter with a "whites only" sign or at the front of the bus.

Study any black-and-white photo from that era and it could double as a fashion shoot. Folks showed up to march and sit in and disrupt in their Sunday best. "That had a lot to do with acceptance," said Agins. "Black people wanted to be accepted. It's not that we were trying to be white, people just wanted to put their best foot forward." Remember the whole baggy pants debate of the 1990s? That was rooted in more than just "these kids today" weaponized nostalgia. For some older African Americans, dressing with your pants hanging down was akin to setting the entire race back a few decades. "That's part of [Maxine's] background, that's part of her makeup," said Givhan. "It was a point of pride that you were able to adhere to the standard." And if not the standard, then better than the status quo. "It's not good enough to be just as good. It's not good enough to meet the requirements, you have to surpass the requirements." This was a lesson Maxine would learn early.

In elementary school in St. Louis, Waters had a teacher who gave the entire classroom marks based on their appearance. Even by the standards of working-class Mill Creek Valley, the Carr-Moore household was struggling. Velma couldn't afford fresh school supplies, much less new clothes for her thirteen children. Little Maxine was fourth in line for girl hand-me-downs, wearing clothes that had already been through the wringer. The girls would fight, she recalled, over who got to wear what when. Regularly, Waters went to school looking anything but polished. "I would get terrible grades because with my mother and all those children you got what you got," said Waters. Every week, Velma rounded the kids up and took them down to the Goodwill. New old clothes arrived on Wednesdays, and the Carr-Moore family would be there to pore over the week's offerings. Maxine quickly learned how to pick the good stuff, how to tell a flimsy dress from a well-made one that would last. Imagine being a little girl who looked up to the elegance and grace embodied in opera singer Grace Bumbry and then having to show up to school each morning looking, in a word, raggedy. It had to be soul-crushing in its way, but for Maxine it was also motivating. Part of the reason Waters got her first real job at thirteen, besides needing to help Velma out at home, was that she wanted to buy her own clothes. "I love clothes. I love clothes a lot."

But how exhausting must all that upkeep, all that sartorial messaging, truly be? It takes time and effort to pull it together day in and day out, especially if you, like the congresswoman, regularly wake up at 5 A.M. and work well past 7 P.M., followed by meme-making cable TV hits past 9 P.M. Does she ever let her hair down? Can she ever show up anywhere not giving the full Maxine? Probably not.

Case in point: Bill O'Reilly, who early one Tuesday morning decided to come for Maxine Waters. On March 28, 2017, the conservative darling known for shouting down guests and settling sexual harassment lawsuits appeared on *Fox and Friends* to plug one of his books. During his segment, O'Reilly was asked to comment on a speech Maxine Waters had given on the House floor the night before. In her address, the congresswoman from California made the case that criticizing the president was patriotic. "When we fight against this president and we point out how dangerous he is for this society and for this country, we're fighting for the democracy," she said. "We're fighting for America. We're saying to those who say they're patriotic, but they've turned a blind eye to the destruction he's about to cause this country: 'You're not nearly as patriotic as we are.'" When asked what he thought of Waters's actual words, O'Reilly couldn't think of anything smart to say, so he said this instead: "I didn't hear a word she said. I was looking at the James Brown wig." Right. A fully grown, allegedly professional media star could not comment intelligently or comprehensively on Waters's political stance, so in an effort to say something, anything, he reached for the lowest common insult, the dumbest thing he could say—*Uhhhh, she looks like a dude.* The insult was idiotic, juvenile, and unfortunately all too familiar to black women in power.

"I think that it was so embedded culturally that when he was grasping for an insult that's where he went," said Givhan. "That he would compare this black woman to a man, that he would pick someone who was known for having crazy hair sometimes, and also picking someone from a specific era who had a reputation for being racially radical?" In short, it was no accident that O'Reilly's mind went there. It's all of a piece. Brown famously sang, "I'm black and I'm proud," in 1968, around the same time Waters was coming into her own politically as a teacher at Head Start. "I think it was meant to not just be an insult, it was meant to denigrate her as a black woman specifically; it just touched on every racial trope there is," said Givhan. And we've seen this before when it comes to black women who dare to be bold and powerful *and* beautiful.

Waters speaks at the 2016 Democratic National Convention in Philadelphia.

Because let's be clear: Maxine looked good when she was schooling folks on what patriotism truly means that evening on the House floor. She was in a royal-looking navy jacket over a matching sheath paired with a chunky silver necklace and her signature red nails and lip. Her hair was laid as usual, not a curl out of place. She looked in charge and that, of course, pisses some people off. Remember when radio host Don Imus infamously called the Rutgers University women's basketball team "nappy-headed hoes"? Or how during her husband's first presidential campaign, conservative news outlets often painted Michelle Obama, a black woman who dared to speak her mind on the campaign trail, as both masculine and militant?

O'Reilly apologized for his "jest" a few hours later, but Waters didn't let that foolishness go unchecked, earning herself another viral moment by appearing on MSNBC that very night with a message: "Let me just say this: I'm a strong black woman and I cannot be intimidated. I cannot be undermined. I cannot be thought to be afraid of Bill O'Reilly or anybody," Waters said on *All In with Chris Hayes.*

She didn't stop there, though: "And I'd like to say to women out there everywhere: Don't allow these right-wing talking heads, these dishonorable people, to intimidate you or scare you. Be who you are. Do what you do. And let us get on with discussing the real issues of this country." Well, okay then. For that TV appearance, she wore a buttery blazer paired with a leopard print choker that cascaded down her chest like chain mail—and that red lip, boo. She did not come to play.

An exultant Waters at a 2017 Prayer Breakfast in Washington, D.C.

"You can be both feminine and wanting to claim your femininity but also recognizing that the strength part is necessary," said Givhan. "It's a complicated stew, and for someone to use this strength part as a weapon against her when it is the very thing that has allowed her to survive and excel . . ." is damaging on a deeper level than just regular everyday Washington mudslinging. The fact that Waters still has to deal with this crap at eighty-one is heartbreaking. The fact that she's still up for the smackdown is inspiring. (Also, O'Reilly got fired less than a month later for continuing to be gross.)

For Davis, that's the secret to Maxine's appeal and her style—being unfazed by outside forces: "She's just the black girl who was never afraid. She's not afraid of Donald Trump and she's not afraid to wear a red lip. It's the same authenticity. She looks like how she feels. That to me is the ultimate stylish person. When you look like what you are."

And Now a Word from the Book of Maxine

So, before Auntie Maxine, there was, in some circles, another nickname. We will speak of this once and then we'll be done with it. Throughout her career, there have been many who have tried to diminish and dismiss Maxine Waters because they didn't know what to make of her. She was impossible to intimidate; she couldn't be talked over. She wouldn't acquiesce to people who had more privilege than her; she gained power of her own against all odds. She was a black woman in white, male-dominated environments who wouldn't let anyone try to put her in her place. So, what's a bigot with a bruised ego to do? Like the playground bully who won't grow up to make anything of himself, some have tried to tear Maxine Waters down with name-calling. Operative word: "tried." Now, Waters is no stranger to, let's say, a descriptive word or two. She's come up with choice nomenclature for all kinds of leaders in her more than forty years in government. But the difference is that any name-calling on her part is always backed up by her beliefs. If Maxine Waters calls you something other than what your parents put on your birth certificate, it's because that's the person she sees in front of her. You might want to do a little self-reflection. And possibly modify your birth certificate.

The same is not true of those who oppose Maxine Waters, which is how the name Kerosene Maxine came to briefly attach itself to her. In a reference to what some regarded as a quick temper and a propensity to ignite situations, right-wing legislators and pundits started tossing it around derisively in the 1990s after her profile rose in the wake of the L.A. insurrection. To be clear, it was intended as an insult, no matter how one feels about Waters's impassioned advocacy. But a strange thing happened: it quickly crossed over into mainstream parlance and lost the edge with which it was crafted. "Kerosene" became a descriptor, popping up in complimentary contexts like a profile in *The Crisis*, the official publication of the NAACP, and news reports on BET through the early 2000s, before fading away as Waters's work on the House Financial Services Committee pulled her out of the spotlight for a while.

The moniker resurfaced around 2016, as Waters emerged as one of the most vociferous voices in the fight against Trump. But it mutated again. Right-wing blogs started to toss it off in spiteful headlines as an insult once more. On the other side, seemingly neutral mentions in wire service articles included it as if it were a piece of biographical detail or a touch of color. Take the following for instance: "She's been called 'Kerosene Maxine' and gaveled off the House floor for accusing Republican men of badgering women." You'd be forgiven for thinking this came from an anti-Maxine blog, but it's actually the lede of a 2019 Associated Press article that positions Waters as a model for freshman Democrats. The name is, now, just another piece of trivia in a long and detailed career. But it's not innocuous.

As with most conservative attacks on her, "Kerosene" never had any corrosive power. But it isn't a term she's reclaimed. In fact, she rejects it. "I think it was born out of a right-wing group's description of a person they didn't like," she told *The New York Times Magazine* in 2017. "They try to tag you with something that would help others believe there's something wrong with you." Whether one sees her fieriness as destructive or as the perfect tool to light bigoted asses up, the word has a more complicated weight to it that will never, fully, pay the representative the respect she's owed. Think of "kerosene" like "explosive," like "out of control," like "raging." This is a word that

A now-iconic image of Waters listening during testimony in 2013.

seeks to burn all the nuance and skill off her powerful rhetoric and her effective advocacy and boil it down to anger. Anger, an emotion some men will label unbecoming of a woman, an out-of-control force, a primal, unsophisticated thing. That's at the root of this word, even when taken out of its insulting context.

"Kerosene" conjures an angry black woman, a stereotype created to disempower passion and to silence volume. Maxine Waters is not a stereotype and she will not be silenced. While she has, on occasion, made a righteous and rightful claim to anger at injustice, the blanket label "angry" is reductive. She put it best in 2017 when she said, "I am an experienced legislator, who understands strategy, who understands the value of speaking truth to power, and I'm not angry as much as I'm determined." And that's all we're going to say about that.

The fact is, however, that Waters is a singular person and a singular leader of uncommon charisma and strength. For years, people have tried to find the right words to describe her. Sometimes those words still dripped with the same bias (unconscious or conscious) that brought "Kerosene Maxine" into the world. Other times they aimed for something higher, a way of capturing her innate dynamism with words. Most times they ended up somewhere between the two points. In any case, all descriptions that try to capture the experience of being in the presence of Maxine Waters are talking about two things at once: the words she

"I'M NOT ANGRY AS MUCH AS I'M **DETERMINED."**

uses and the way she uses them. So, in this brief diversion, we're not talking about nicknames so much as we are trying to name the powerful and somewhat ineffable.

When Augustus F. Hawkins handpicked Waters to succeed him as the congressperson representing what was then California's 29th Congressional District in 1990, there was little doubt that she would have an easy path to victory. Though she worked hard for it, as we detailed earlier, her self-confidence was earned and has been borne out by history. In the run-up to the election, she told the *Essence* board of directors, on which she sat, "I've got it made and I have a seat at the table already." This wasn't empty chest-puffing. This was an experienced fifty-two-year-old legislator who had already raised $470,000 for her campaign and was taking the next step in an already powerful career. At least, that's what it looks like in retrospect. Something must have been wrong with some people's eyeglasses prescriptions back in the day, though, because not everyone shared Waters's confidence. One Washington-based lobbyist who was reached by the *Los Angeles Times* conceded that she was a powerhouse articulator of ideas, but he guessed she would have a hard time adjusting to Congress. "I think she's going to have to file the sharp edge of her tongue a little bit if she wants to get along." The lobbyist retained his anonymity, probably because if he hadn't, we'd be outside his house right now.

File the sharp edge of her tongue if she wants to get along. The temerity. The brazen misogyny. The complete misunderstanding of Maxine Waters. She's not here to "get along" (which is really code for "shut up and step back"); she's here to get things done. This lobbyist really fixed his mouth to say that Maxine Waters needed to perform metaphorical surgery on her tongue if she wanted anyone to listen to her, and while that's shocking, it's also indicative of the way that people throughout her career have tried to understand her by fitting her into a box that they created instead of reckoning with her on her own terms.

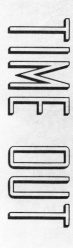

In this respect, the most illustrative (and sometimes most damning) evidence comes not from pitiful nicknames or from anonymous sniping, but from supposedly impartial words that journalists have plucked out of dog-eared thesauruses and inserted into the papers of record. Looking back over Waters's thousands of media mentions, you notice that for the first fifteen years of her career, there was an insistent tradition of using a telling adjective in nearly every article to help readers truly get who she was. Or, we should say, who the writer thought she was. Part of this is standard practice, particularly for figures whom the average reader may not know well. It drops off outside of colorful profiles midway through the 1990s. People knew Maxine Waters then; they had their own adjectives. But the way that she was framed prior to ascension to the level of national awareness says a lot about the time and the context that she had to push back against.

Here's a selection:

"tiny, energetic" —Daily Union Democrat, October 9, 1979

This is one of her first mentions and it's more neutral than those that would come later. The words create an interesting juxtaposition that hints at a contradiction. "She's small but also she has energy. Can you believe it?" This doesn't, on the surface, seek to diminish her but it does treat her as a bit of a novelty. Would someone then, or now, write the same of, say, Michael Bloomberg, who at 5'8" is five inches shorter than the average president? The writer is reaching for a description here that would get pulled in many different directions over the next decade. But this is a good place to start: she possesses energy and power and there's something about it that is surprising. Perhaps Waters's own words, from an interview more than forty years later, can help illuminate this aspect of her personality: "As an African American woman who has been involved in the struggle, you know it's coming, you know who they are, and you know how not to let it devastate you. And you build the strength to fight back, to push back, and let it just go over your shoulders, you know it's not something that's going to put me in the bed. Every day I wake up, I wake up energized."

"dynamic"—*Eugene Register-Guard,* June 2, 1980

A rare adjective that seems totally unencumbered by secondary ideas about race or gender. From the Greek word *dunamis,* which means "power." It is, perhaps, the best way to describe her presence. "Dynamic," when used as a noun, means "a force that causes change in a system," which is exactly the way she's operated in her career. As an adjective it means, among other things, "constantly changing or active" and also "positive or lively."

"outspoken"—*Afro-American,* October 13, 1984

There seems little doubt that Waters is fearless with her pronouncements, and so, perhaps, "outspoken" is a reasonable term for her. But let's just pull the thread a little. To be outspoken, one has to be speaking more than is expected or allowed. Is it reasonable, then, to expect an elected leader not to speak out? Or is it possible this compliment is rooted in an assumption of meekness? And where might that assumption come from?

"able and articulate"—*Afro-American,* March 30, 1985

It's interesting that these two terms—which context suggests should be read positively—come from the *Afro-American,* a newspaper produced by and for the black community since 1982, because the word "articulate" has been used as a backhanded compliment or a microaggression against black people for years. Often, when a nonblack person speaks highly of a black person by calling them articulate, it's meant genuinely but it

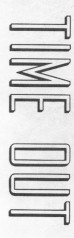

suggests that being able to speak clearly or communicate effectively is an anomaly. This connects to larger prejudices around black people regarding speech and intelligence, the basic idea being the untrue, negative stereotype that black people are not as intelligent and a "nontraditional" speech pattern is evidence of that. Perhaps the most notorious recent example of this comes from 2007, when then senator Joe Biden was preparing for his presidential run. "You got the first mainstream African-American who is articulate and bright and clean and a nice-looking guy. I mean, that's a storybook, man," Biden said of then senator Barack Obama, his rival for the Democratic nomination, in an interview with the *New York Observer*. Biden called Obama with an apology, which Obama publicly accepted while noting "Biden's comments were historically inaccurate. African-American presidential candidates like Jesse Jackson, Shirley Chisholm, Carol Mosely Braun, and Al Sharpton gave a voice to many important issues through their campaigns, and no one would call them inarticulate."

The term remains a potential minefield not for its surface meaning, but for the underlying assumptions that make it notable for some and worthy of comment. None of that is at play here, thankfully, as we get to appreciate the adjective in a genuine state. Maxine Waters is uniquely adept at articulating her thoughts and beliefs; she's a master communicator. She's one of the best public speakers alive. That's what we're seeing communicated here.

"opinionated and daring" —*Ebony,* August 1984

Like the *Facts of Life* theme song says, "You take the good, you take the bad, you take the rest, and there you have . . ." well, this description. "Daring" has positive connotations that aren't tied to race or gender, but rather leadership qualities. But "opinionated" is an interesting choice here, as it is generally not a positive way of talking about someone who has thoughts in her head.

"feisty" —*Los Angeles Times,* May 19, 1985

Yikes. A lot to unpack here. "Feisty" is a term almost exclusively applied to women, often used to describe a spiritedness that, while not "unladylike," is, in the context, unusual. Feistiness is a sister to pluck or spunk. It's not negative, but as with the word "articulate," one should ask what the presumption behind the compliment is. Also, not for nothing, but the origin of the word is *fist,* a Middle English word for a small dog. Why are we using this word?

"aggressive" —*Los Angeles Times,* May 22, 1988

Look how much things change in three short years, almost to the day. In the same paper she's gone from feisty to aggressive, which seems to be a case of saying the quiet part out loud. The descriptions stop being anomalies and start being commentaries hereafter.

"combative" —*Los Angeles Times,* October 6, 1989

A level up from aggressive. She is at the height of her powers in the California Assembly and about to launch into Congress. Soon some misguided soul will suggest, anonymously, that she file the sharp edge of her tongue down. In many ways, the very much not anonymous newspaper in which this word appeared associated with her name is suggesting the same thing. "Combative" is a word used to describe an antagonist, a fight starter, someone who doesn't get along. This is a word used to put someone on the outside of a system, to call attention to a lack of decorum. This word polices. This same year, she reflected on the impression that others had of her and gently, but wisely, made it clear that any problems with her style were problems of the listeners' comprehension and not her communication. "The image of being tough that I got here was created because I was tough in an atmosphere that had never seen a black woman work," she said at the time. "That's the way of life for us, that's the way we talk to each other. In my neighborhood where I was raised, we didn't consider it unkind or, as they say, aggressive. What I considered natural and acceptable became aggressive, confrontational, all kinds of things."

"Assertive and powerful" —*Ebony,* October 1992

Again, the black press is able to capture something about Waters that in other instances has bound mainstream press up in knots and left it flummoxed. "Assertive" is in the same family as "aggressive," but it doesn't police. It presupposes that speaking up for oneself is unusual,

Waters, with Jesse Jackson, speaks at a Los Angeles Board of Supervisors hearing in 2004.

but it doesn't seem to be bogged down by assumptions about race or gender. "Powerful" is another neutral but accurate description. In 1992 she was powerful; she advised a future president and had the ear of Jesse Jackson; she challenged the sitting president openly and called him a racist. She was full of power.

"irrepressible" —Los Angeles Times, May 16, 1993

Of all the words—positive, negative, neutral—that have been used to describe Maxine Waters, "irrepressible" is perhaps not the most on the nose, but it does have a lot of meta-textual resonance. She can't be repressed or oppressed by adjectives; she is always going to be bigger than mere words.

MAXINE'S WORDS

In addition to the tone of her speech and the content of her speech, what makes a pronouncement from Maxine Waters most dynamic is the style of her speech. She has a way with words like no other. There's her voice—throaty and strong, like a pastor's—and her enunciation—crisper than a new hundred-dollar bill, like a schoolteacher's; oh, and don't forget her cadence—Maxine Waters has a flow that could rival those of all the rappers she's befriended over the years. There's a musicality to the way Waters speaks, with the slightest hint of the honeyed tones of her St. Louis roots, the sounds of black voices coming from all across the South and converging in the middle of the country to speak a new life into existence. Whether she's delivering prepared remarks on the floor of the House or giving an off-the-cuff quip to a reporter, Waters captivates. She's a natural orator. A raconteur. And, like many politicians, a master at staying on message. We haven't reached 2020 yet in this book, but just think about how a certain president speaks in comparison. Just imagine his two brain

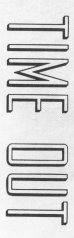

cells struggling to string together a sentence and then compare it to the brilliance and beauty that regularly pours forth from Maxine Waters. You don't want to be caught in a verbal sparring match with this one; you will always lose, but at least it'll sound great while it happens.

One of the most delightful experiences, if you can swing it, is to catch the congresswoman in conversation, whether in a constituent visit, a conversation, or a podcast interview. It's in these exchanges that you get to see all the parts of her public self—the orator, the strategist, the wisecracking quipster, and the leader. You also get to see her natural style of marrying clauses and sentences, something that can sometimes get lost in prepared remarks that may have passed through the hands of a couple staff members first. Let's—just for fun—hang out for a bit with one such snippet and see what it tells us. This is from an interview with Eric in her office in Washington, D.C., in December 2017.

DETERMINED

For someone whose rhetoric is so often misconstrued or purposefully misunderstood, making herself clear is crucial. Additionally, as someone who has spent more than forty years giving speeches, she also knows that old marketing adage that you have to see (or, in this case, hear) something three times for it to make an impact.

Even more than repetition, however, Waters employs lists. She *loves* a list.

YOU KNOW WHAT I'M TOLD?

This phrase has the folksy familiarity that could precede anything from good gossip to ancient wisdom. It draws you in.

I'm absolutely **DETERMINED**. I will not sit idly by and allow the president of the United States to disrespect so many people, to lie to us, and to dog whistle to the white nationalists, and the KKK, and the white supremacists. And so, I'm determined, and I have the energy, and I have the will, and it's not anger as much as it is a kind of toughness and willing to fight.

YOU KNOW WHAT I'M TOLD? I'm told that there are so many people out there who believe they don't have power, that they don't have influence, and what they have to say doesn't make a difference. I would like, in the best way possible, to support people being able to think of themselves as people with influence and power. And so I don't like people to feel hopeless, or they can't make a difference. You know, I love this story about . . . I guess up in Virginia, as of today, somebody won by one vote. Did you see that? That's an example, and I hope people see that, because I do think people have power if they learn to use it. **THEY HAVE THE POWER** to write, they have the power to email, they have the power to telephone, they have the power to organize their neighborhood, they have the power to go to their church and tell the minister, "Why can't we have a community meeting here every week so that we can educate people?" And so, I think people have a lot of power. And when they get in touch with that power then they will activate, they will do things, and I think everybody can do that.

First, a little bit of context: 2017, as you'll read in a little bit, had been a year of explosive public awareness for Waters. She'd gone viral a couple of times in quick succession for her sharp critiques of the president and former FBI director James Comey. She had also come out victorious in a verbal tussle at a House Financial Services Committee hearing with Treasury secretary Steve Mnuchin during which she repeatedly exercised the procedural option to reclaim her time (that phrase is so familiar . . . wonder why . . .). Maxine Waters was in high demand and on fire. She spent a lot of 2017 embracing her newly minted status as a millennial icon by giving stump speeches and interviews about her calls to impeach the president. That's the energy that undergirds the quote above.

This selection comes right after words quoted earlier in this chapter: "I am an experienced legislator, who understands strategy, who understands the value of speaking truth to power, and I'm not angry as much as I'm **DETERMINED**." Adding that back in, it's notable that her speech pattern uses rhythmic repetition both within sentences and

What is the function of a list? For one, cadence: a list interrupts the rhythm of a paragraph and wraps the listener in a new rhythm, albeit temporarily. It's like a spell or the bridge in a song. It grabs your attention. It also allows the speaker to expand on a single point, thereby complicating her ideas and adding depth without cluttering the message. Each list splits off from the main idea like a branch on a tree, but the trunk remains the same. In this case, the trunk is the idea of her determination.

from one sentence to the next. In the first three sentences the word "determined" pops up. This isn't accidental. She was asked about whether she was angry about the state of the country; she wanted to make it clear that determination was the phrase that pays.

That determination then pivots to a call to action, which is masterful. She's been asked to reveal something about her emotional state, but what use is that to her, or to her cause? As a legislator she knows that nothing happens without buy-in and that her voice is the stand-in for thousands, millions even. And so she turns the attention back on us. She's determined; how are we feeling? If the answer is "Not so inspired," she's got good news for us in the form of an anecdote about someone who won their election by one vote—a true event with a clear takeaway: your determination matters and can make a difference.

How does she get us there? By asking a question and then providing an answer like this. When she transitions away from talking about herself, she does so by identifying a problem and then immediately proposing a solution. A question also reminds the listener that they are in conversation and that she is aware of their presence. It's a check-in. Additionally, there is the question "You know what I'm told?"

Another tool of the trade—a common one employed by politicians—is introducing rhetorical dialogue. In this case, she models a constituent talking to a minister and asking, "Why can't we have a community meeting here every week so that we can educate people?" This kind of modeling is a handy tool for Waters because it simultaneously puts her in her constituents' shoes and makes her an example for them. It, too, is a kind of spell, promising "If you say the words I'm saying, you can also attain the power I'm offering you."

This, essentially, is the root of her rhetoric and of her leadership style. She is a natural coach, a teacher. She is trying to share knowledge and share resources; she is not being stingy with her power. She knows that when her constituents are powerful, or when anyone with whom she is speaking is able to plug into a source of their own power because of it, it can bring only benefits. The charming paradox is that though no one speaks like Maxine, everything works better when we take heed and take heart of Waters's words.

CHAPTER TEN

"I'M NOT AFRAID OF ANYBODY"

2016–2020

IN WHICH IT IS SHOWN HOW REPRESENTATIVE
MAXINE WATERS TAKES ON THE PRESIDENT AND THE
"KREMLIN KLAN" AND THE OTHERS RUN FOR COVER

f Representative Maxine Waters's life were a Shonda Rhimes prime-time drama (and, by the by, Shonda, if you're reading this, it definitely should be), President Trump would loom over the later seasons as the Big Bad. You know the Big Bad—the shady character who emerges from the periphery, the puppet master who is revealed to be behind some of the most dastardly and complex acts of treachery, the villain whom the hero has been training all her life to face. And defeat. This would be a show in which a former Head Start teacher, who rose in the political world through determination, grit, and the unobstructed will of the people, ends up head-to-head with the leader of the free world in a battle for the nation. And in some ways, that's reality. Except . . . Well, you're familiar with Donald Trump, right? This man is, indeed, the leader of the free world and he does, in later seasons, find himself unfortunately in Representative Waters's crosshairs. But this is not a fair fight. This isn't the clash of two equals, one on the side of truth, justice, and opportunity and the other, well, you know. Maxine Waters may have faced down men like Trump who manifested systemic oppression and discounted her voice for her entire career, but the forty-fifth president is by no means the worst of them. Maxine Waters did not work her whole life just to get on MSNBC and take down an inarticulate real estate flimflam man.

So, is this a final showdown that the rules of drama demand? Well, we may have to take a rain check on that. First of all, you'd be lucky to even get Maxine Waters in the same room as him. And he'd be lucky, too, to be graced with her presence. But don't hold your breath. Asked once what she would say to Trump if they had a private conversation, she had a quick and curt reply: "I would not waste my time." Bloop. That time? Reclaimed it, wouldn't waste it; next question.

It is, honestly, a shame that a career as storied and accomplished as Maxine Waters's has to be sullied with the presence of a minor character like the former host of *The Apprentice*. Come on, now; the man is not on her level. Even he knows it. Sure, he lashes out at her and sends his lackeys out to call her names. But she will outspeak him, outmaneuver him, and outpolitic him at every turn. She's not new to this; she's true to this. She has never lost an election. He has never won a popular vote. Why are we even having this conversation? Yes, Donald Trump is president of the United States of America. And? He is not Maxine Waters's Big Bad.

In the modern Maxine era, that "him" with whom she had no interest in being involved could have been one of many people. There's been a whole career of "hims" who turned out to have forfeited the battle before it was even begun. Dudes who have officially tried it with Maxine Waters even though her middle name may as well be "Don't Try It." So, instead of a final battle to cap off an illustrious career of telling the truth and taking no prisoners, how about a victory lap? A retrospective of regrettables, a tale of squalls that thought they were hurricanes and the waters that remained, as ever, undisturbed. For, as she herself will tell you, Maxine Waters is not afraid of anybody.

THE TEA PARTY

CNN's Van Jones called the election of Donald Trump the "whitelash" against President Barack Obama, but it's arguable that that outsize, hysterical pushback started far before 2016. Some would say the first flareups began in 2009, with the creation of the Tea Party, an ostensibly "fiscally conservative" offshoot of the Republican Party that couldn't quite seem to shake the rumor that it was undergirded by dog whistle racism and a bigoted reaction to the Obama presidency. A 2010 survey by the University of Washington Institute for the Study of Ethnicity, Race & Sexuality found that Tea Party supporters were 25 percent more likely to be racially resentful than nonsupporters. A *New York Times*/CBS News poll the same year found that Tea Partiers—who made up 18 percent of the population at the time—felt that Obama did not share American values. The poll also showed that Tea Party supporters were more likely than the general public to feel "too much has been made of the problems facing blacks."

It may have been born out of a protest of an economic stimulus package, but the Tea Party was raised by old-fashioned American prejudice. Maxine Waters knew that; she could see it plain as day, and she was more than willing to help this party (the kind of party with terrible music and a cash bar) shuffle off this mortal coil.

Though Waters supported the work of President Obama, she didn't feel any compunction not to be critical of him when she felt his actions demanded it. And 2011, as he prepared to face off with a Tea Party at the height of its popularity and a Republican challenge from John McCain and, if you can believe it, Sarah Palin, was just such a time. "The president is going to have to fight and he's going to have to fight hard," she told CBS. "The Congressional Black Caucus loves the president. We're supportive of the president, but we're getting tired."

A few days later, she attended an event called the Kitchen Table Summit in California and told the crowd there, "I'm not afraid of the big bad wolf. I'm not afraid of anybody. This is a tough game. You can't be intimidated. You can't be frightened." She punctuated every phrase with a powerful wave of her hand like a blessing over the thousand-person crowd. Like she was casting out a demon. Because, real talk, she was. In a fitted white blazer and black slacks, she cut a typically striking and powerful figure. She roamed the stage, microphone in hand, intense in her passion and holding the crowd in the palm of her hand. She ramped up to the climax of her spell: "And as far as I'm concerned, the Tea Party can go straight to hell!" The crowd went wild, standing, hooting, cheering. She waited, knowing that she wasn't quite done, but she needed to let them get their whole lives before she hit them with the zinger. Finally, she straightened her jacket and concluded: "*And* I intend to help them get there." This last part she tossed off with the full confidence of a stand-up comedian who has just brought the house down and is now just stunting on them. The crowd lost their minds.

There's nothing new to this brand of Maxine Waters truth-telling, but because she'd been out of the spotlight and working on the House Financial Services Committee for a while, folks started acting brand-new and the comments generated a lot of press. Not to say that this moment isn't deserving of attention on its own, of course. A congresswoman talking about not just defeating or dismantling a rogue arm of a political party but sending it straight to hell? That's some spicy stuff. Not sending it to sit in the corner, not sending it down to the minor leagues. No. Not sending it back to the lab, sending it to charm school, sending it out on an ice floe. To hell. The Tea Party can proceed straight to hell, do not pass Go, do not collect two hundred devil dollars. With a return address label that reads "The Office of Maxine Waters, Real One."

The Tea Party did not end up slow dancing on the flames, per se, but it definitely fell out of favor and power midway through Obama's second term and hasn't been heard from since. For an attention-hungry activist arm, that is about as close to hell as it comes.

Cut to Maxine Waters walking slowly away from the dumpster fire, still in a pristine white jacket, and decisively dropping the mic.

THE KREMLIN KLAN

If you know what's good for you, you never miss Maxine Waters on MSNBC's *All In with Chris Hayes*. The host, who has the energy of a grown 'n' sexy Harry Potter, is the perfect counterpoint and straight man to Waters's fire hose of energy. In her frequent appearances on the show, Waters goes, as the title says, all in on whatever the topic du jour is as Hayes blinks back shock, surprise, and amusement at the barrage of words. Does he attempt to get a word in edgewise? Sometimes, but he knows better than to push it too far. One of Waters's greatest appearances occurred on February 21, 2017, during a segment titled simply "Trump & The Russians." In a six-minute segment, Waters brought more fire than the entirety of the movie *Backdraft* with a monologue that would make *Scandal*'s Olivia Pope blush. Her objective: to take down the "scumbags" she succinctly called the "Kremlin Klan," a group of Trump associates who were believed to be in league with Russian interests associated with President Vladimir Putin.

You know that scene in a John Grisham novel where the lead lawyer brings the case to a devastating close with a soul-stirring, roof-raising closing argument in the largest courthouse in the county? Well, imagine that, but instead of a lawyer it's a septuagenarian in a periwinkle jacket displaying a smile that says, "Y'all are not ready for this." Maxine Waters's appearance on *All In* went beyond a media hit, beyond courtroom argument, and ascended to a full-blown testimony. Like the crowd at the Kitchen Table Summit six year earlier, you will watch it and you will get your entire life.

In the middle of the appearance, Waters stopped speaking directly to the camera (which was a small mercy, as the intensity of her gaze makes one think, "Maybe *I* colluded with Russia too?") and pulled out a pair of spectacles and a list of names. A. List. Of. Names. She went from reading for filth to just plain reading. What was on this list? All the names of the people she considered part of the Kremlin Klan. All the people whom, may we remind you, she described to Hayes as "scumbags." Honey, Maxine Waters did not come to play, did not accept your calendar request for play time, and does not foresee playing to be in the cards on this day. She brought a list and her glasses, y'all. She was a one-woman Library of Congress and she came to read. She was trying to single-handedly wake the country up to the peril that she saw, and if that meant pulling out a folded piece of paper on live television like Martin Luther at the doors of the church, then so be it!

A few months later, she'd give her definition of "patriotism," which was "whether or not you will defend your democracy and what it's supposed to stand for. And whether or not you will fight to strengthen it." So, while the *All In* appearance is a show worthy of its own prime-time hour, it is also an act of patriotism. And patriotism never sounded so good.

JAMES COMEY

Oh dear. Do you remember James Comey? The very tall man who was once the director of the FBI before getting caught in Donald Trump's deranged crosshairs and getting dismissed midway through 2017? Comey was criticized by both sides, for different reasons, regarding his handling of the Russian interference in the 2016 election and the investigation (which ultimately proved baseless)

Waters speaks to a crowd at a rally against a GOP tax plan in 2017.

into Hillary Clinton's emails, Trump decided to fire Comey in May 2017—supposedly on the advice of then attorney general Jeff Sessions and then deputy attorney general Rod Rosenstein (both of whom later resigned out of the pervasive cloud of Trump administration ignominy). Comey's rocky relationship with the Trump administration set off a series of events that really should have brought this whole imbroglio to a screeching halt, but, of course did not. It did produce some dramatic moments in American history and present Comey as both a hero and a villain at alternate times and in alternate lights. But nothing was more dramatic than the twenty-one seconds that Maxine Waters spent giving her highly unfavorable opinion about him. And, frankly, after Maxine Waters gives you the tea, what use do you have for other opinions?

A group of congressional leaders met with Comey just prior to Trump's administration to get information on Russian meddling in the election and the investigation into the same. To put it mildly, it did not go well. Waters emerged from the closed-door meeting and addressed a roomfull of reporters. Well, "addressed" is the wrong word. She allowed a roomful of reporters to be in her presence. Begrudgingly. She started the press conference, one of many she's given over the course of her life, not by giving a prepared statement but by staring with pursed lips over the gathered throng and then eventually asking, "Yes . . . Can I help you? What do you want?" with all the annoyance of a grandparent who wants you to know that you're stomping on her last nerve.

Waters had *already* had it before a single word was said. This level of open exasperation is truly a marvel in this era of packaged, focus-grouped statements and canned responses. It would come to define this time in American politics. But it wasn't even as over it as Waters would get in this appearance.

"What do you want?" This is the kind of question and tone that, if you know what's good for you, you have a good and quick answer for. A reporter finally mustered the courage to ask Waters, "How did it go today?" That was, apparently, not what Waters was looking for, as she gave the pithy response, "It went fine." The level of pregnant pauses in this press conference had reached Pinter levels by this point.

Another reporter pressed forward, getting a piece of a question out: "Can you tell us anything about the discussion in the—" But Waters chose this glorious moment to reveal the true breadth of her magnificent exasperation. She cut the question off and replied, "No, it's classified and we can't tell you anything." A news conference with no news! This is *art* and we need to hang it in the Louvre. Waters continued, ferociously: "All I can tell you is that the FBI director has *no credibility*," and as she tossed the last two words into the room like she was throwing egg shells in the garbage disposal, she flung her hands at the crowd dismissively and stalked away from the mics. This is, without hyperbole, the greatest press conference ever held. We learn nothing, and yet we have all the information we need to carry on forever.

DONALD TRUMP

"You know what?" Waters told the *New York Times* in 2017. "I'm taking the gloves off and I'm going to step out. . . . [Trump is] a

Waters protests the count of the electoral votes in the 2016 election in a joint session of Congress.

bully, an egotistical maniac, a liar, and someone who did not need to be president." Oh, those gloves were *off* off. There's a reason that Trump isn't included in the Time Out about the presidents: Representative Waters has never viewed him with anything more than derision because of the things that he has said and the shameless way that he has behaved, even before he officially took office. Trump was beneath the presidency and beneath her level as well. What can we say about Donald Trump that is better than Waters's reasoning for not attending his inauguration: "I don't honor him. I don't respect him. And I don't want to be involved with him." Simple, succinct, put it on a T-shirt.

She's called him a "disgusting, poor excuse of a man."

She tweeted, "Impeachment is not good enough for Trump. He needs to be imprisoned & placed in solitary confinement."

She declared, "He's embarrassing us every day." The list goes on and on.

You could, honestly, make a daily calendar with a different Maxine Waters Trump takedown on each page. Maxine Waters has never taken anything more than a dim view of this man, whom she describes as the worst she's ever seen. "I think he believes in nothing," she said in a 2017 interview. "I think he cares about nothing." And nothing is exactly all that this book owes him. He's not worthy of taking up space or time in the story of Maxine Waters. Consider it reclaimed.

A FINAL WORD FROM THE BOOK OF MAXINE

On December 18, 2019, the House voted to impeach Trump for abuse of power and obstruction of Congress. Prior to the vote, Waters strode to the podium and gave a fiery, impassioned speech in which she reiterated Trump's misdeeds and her own case, reminding people that she'd been saying he's no good from day one and welcoming them all to catch up.

MAXINE WATERS'S HOUSE FLOOR SPEECH, DECEMBER 18, 2019

Ladies and gentlemen, unfortunately the rules of debate won't allow me to cite all of the reasons why this President should be impeached; there are many. However, Madam Speaker and members of this House, to quote the late Maya Angelou, "when someone shows you who they are, believe them the first time." This day was not inevitable, but it was predictable because this president has shown himself time and time again to believe that he is above the law and he has no respect for our Constitution or our democracy. Based on all that we know about Donald Trump, we could have predicted he would have abused the power of the president by corruptly soliciting the government of Ukraine and the Ukrainian president Volodymyr Zelensky to publicly announce investigations into his political opponent, former vice president Joseph R. Biden. This impeachment resolution includes evidence that this president withheld $391 million of taxpayer funds that Congress appropriated for the purpose of providing vital military and security assistance to Ukraine to oppose Russian aggression. Another blatant abuse of power.

Waters at the Women's Convention in October 2017.

Our investigations revealed that this president advanced a discredited theory, promoted by Russia, alleging that Ukraine rather than Russia interfered in the 2016 United States presidential election for corrupt purposes in pursuit of personal political benefit. Never before in our history have we experienced a president who has so clearly conducted himself in a manner offensive to and subversive of the Constitution, and directed his cabinet members, executive branch agencies, and other White House officials to defy lawful subpoenas from Congress. Was he attempting to hide wrongdoing? It is without question that this president has demonstrated that he will remain a threat to national security and the

Constitution if allowed to remain in office and has acted in
a manner grossly incompatible with self-governance and the
rule of law, because at every turn he has shown us who he is.

It is no secret that the president could have been
impeached a long time ago. Today, we stand here with
an irrefutable case and an indisputable set of facts that
this president absolutely abused his power and obstructed
Congress. Any other individual who would have been
caught conducting themselves in the way this president has
would have been prosecuted to the full extent of the law. It
is shameful that any members of this House are willing to
disregard the Constitution, turn a blind eye to hard facts,
and ignore a confession from the president himself. History
will remember those who were willing to speak truth to
power. Yes, I called for Trump's impeachment early! *This*
is our country! Our foremothers and forefathers shed their
blood to build and defend this democracy. I refuse to have it
undermined. I wholeheartedly support this resolution. I'm
proud that in the final analysis justice will have been served
in America and Donald Trump will have been impeached!

"HISTORY will REMEMBER
THOSE WHO WERE WILLING TO
SPEAK TRUTH TO POWER."

Amen.

CHAPTER ELEVEN

FINAL THOUGHTS

IN WHICH WE, THE AUTHORS, TELL YOU,
DEAR READER, HOW WE REALLY FEEL

FROM HELENA:

I like living in a world where there's a Maxine Waters.

The congresswoman reminds me so much of my grandmother Frenchie Mae Andrews. Born ten years before Maxine, she was whip smart and suffered not one fool. She was a tiny lion with a shot glass personality. She went down smooth—she never screamed, she never shouted—but, man oh man, you would feel it the next day.

While spending time researching Maxine Waters, I couldn't help but think back to my grandmother, who died in 2015. She lived in Waters's district for decades. I never got to ask her but I am sure she saw a lot of herself in the congresswoman. Married young, moved to Los Angeles in the 1950s in search of something better. But unlike Waters, my grandmother didn't have her aha moment until later in life, when she ditched her husband, raised her kids, and then started traveling. In her seventies she sold hot dogs and chili Fritos from a cart off Vermont Avenue and eventually opened a soul food restaurant. But what if? What if she had grabbed some space for herself earlier in life? What could she have accomplished as well? What could she have meant to the world and not just the dozens of us who share her face? How awesome, then, is it that there is a woman in the U.S. House of Representatives who embodies so many of the attributes of my grandmommy and is being celebrated for it?

So, that's the biggest lesson Waters taught me. Figure yourself out, girl. Don't just accept what life hands you—poverty, too few opportunities, the paralyzing responsibility of raising tiny humans—and do the obvious thing. Do the bold thing. Discover yourself like Maxine did at Head Start. Figure out what you like and what you don't like. Are you being silenced? Are you a pleaser? Want to change all that? Good. It's not too late. This woman found out she wanted something different and went after it—attending college ten years after graduating from high school, digging into her career another ten years after that, and still in the trenches a half a century later. There is no blueprint besides "Do you." And that's why Maxine Waters is more than a meme or a wink or an auntie. She's a constant reminder of what happens when you stop caring about what other people think and start giving a damn about what you think.

FROM ERIC:

I started out as a fan. And a late one at that. The first time I became aware of the seemingly supernatural force that is Representative Maxine Waters was in a twenty-second video clip on Facebook, the one when she trashed her entire meeting with James Comey and read him for filth with a few choice words. I was immediately obsessed. I wrote about her in my daily pop culture and politics humor column on ELLE.com. At one point I wrote that, hyperbolically, I had never seen anything like this outside of a family reunion, likening her to that one auntie we all have who got rich selling Avon and has the good gossip. To my total surprise, that article went viral and the nickname Auntie Maxine started popping up around the Internet. Then, to my great relief, the representative herself took ownership of it. "You're so wonderful!" she tweeted to me in July 2017. (Yes, I'm bragging, but when you have receipts like this, you have to. It's the law.) "B/C of you, Auntie Maxine exists. Your writing gets more special and creative every time!"

While I greatly appreciated her compliments, I was—and continue to be—awed by her work, her words, and her wit. I was honored that she accepted my enthusiastic, humorous take on her in the spirit in which it was offered and that honor only deepened as I actually learned who it was I was writing about.

Growing up in Baltimore in the 1980s and 1990s, I had the pleasure of touring the Capitol and meeting Representatives Kweisi Mfume and Elijah Cummings, both of whom loomed large in our district. My parents made clear how remarkable it was to be represented by black people, how crucial it was to vote, to take political action, and, when needed, to make sure our representatives heard from us when they weren't doing things we agreed with. The political process was a dialogue; it was our right and the hard-won inheritance that generations of black activists and leaders had fought for. I learned not to take it lightly, as an American and particularly as a black American.

I didn't know then about the work that Representative Waters had been putting in across the country and also in D.C. since before I was born. I didn't know about how hard she worked to seek out and hear the voices of her constituency, particularly the most marginalized. I didn't know how deftly she leveraged her unique style, her take-no-prisoners stance, and her magnificent way with words in service of the task she'd been elected to perform: represent.

Maxine Waters does not represent my district, but, humbly, I believe she represents me. She is an example for me of what we can be as Americans, as black people, as lovers of words, and as the shapers of the future. I am proud to live at the same time as her, and I hope that our words here can lead others to a deeper engagement with their own agency in the American political process and a greater appreciation of the incredible Maxine Waters.

MAXINE IN THE MEDIA

We are blessed to be living in the golden age of Maxine media and merch. You'll find Waters on your TV, in your GIF library, trick-or-treating at your house, on products on shelves, and, of course, in your local bookstore. We are minutes from a Maxine Waters Cinematic Universe and theme park. There's no limit to how big Maxine Mania can get. Let's take a look at some of the myriad ways Representative Waters has popped up in pop culture, public art, and even prayer candles.

THE VIEW

On August 4, 2017, singer Mykal Kilgore, who'd recently gone viral with a YouTube video of him singing an original song based on the "reclaiming my time" back and forth, surprised Waters on *The View* with a command performance. Maxine memes were now inspiring art; we may get a Maxine musical before all is said and done.

Singer Mykal Kilgore performs his original song inspired by Representative Waters on *The View.*

"RECLAIMING MY TIME: GOSPEL REMIX" BY MYKAL KILGORE

You want to talk about the things I've done but
I'm reclaiming my time!
You want to speak on the battles I've won but
I'm reclaiming my time!
That's not why I brought you here to share and
I'm reclaiming my time!
Don't read my resume cuz I was there
I'm reclaiming my time!
Oooo
I'm reclaiming
My time!
Yes I am!
My time!
Every minute!
My time!
Every second!
My time!
Stop talking,
My time!
You know the rules,
My time!
When it's my time,
My time!
I can take it back,
Oooooo
What about the letter
Reclaiming my time!
That I sent you way back when
Reclaiming my time!
Give me the answer to the question
Reclaiming my time!
Or don't open your mouth again
Reclaiming my time!
Reclaiming, Reclaiming, Reclaiming
Ooooo
I'm reclaiming my time!

A Denver mural by Thomas Evans.

Maxine Waters–themed street art in Washington, D.C.

MAXINE IN THE MEDIA

A Maxine-themed Rosh Hashanah.

A model rocks a Maxine Waters–
themed shirt by Willy Chavarria.

Dr. Christina Thomas's Waters-quoting
graduation cap.

A Maxine Waters greeting card by Etsy store
This Girl's Just Sayin'.

On an episode of the short-lived sitcom *The Mayor*, a character played by Yvette Nicole Brown joined the zeitgeist and went as the popular representative for Halloween. She wasn't alone. When Maxine Mania reached its zenith in 2017 and 2018, trick-or-treaters all over the nation were donning their best reading glasses and reclaiming their candy.

Eighteen-month-old Carmen as Maxine for Halloween.

ACKNOWLEDGMENTS

This book has been in the making since August 15, 1938, when one Maxine Carr was born. Her book was being written from the very start. But it wouldn't be here now in your hands if it wasn't for the vision of Alessandra Bastagli.

From the beginning, everyone at Dey Street Books believed that this book was not just a good idea but a necessary one. Without the indefatigable efforts of Rosy Tahan, Peter Kispert, Anna Brill, Kendra Newton, Alison Hinchcliffe, and Tatiana Dubin, this book wouldn't be possible. Writing, publishing, and promoting a book under any circumstance is an uphill battle, doing so during a global pandemic is a near impossible task. These folks made it look easy.

Working with the incredibly talented Sabrina Dorsainvil to bring the visuals of this book to life was a privilege and added much-needed inspiration.

Representative Waters's congressional staff, particularly Rykia Dorsey and Twaun Samuel, provided invaluable help and guidance throughout this process. They do an incredible service for this country, and we're grateful that they made time for us in their very busy schedules.

FROM HELENA

I was six weeks postpartum when we started writing this book, so first and foremost I have to thank my sister-in-law, Jaimy Snow, who came from Nebraska to Washington, D.C., to care for my baby while I was holed up in the upstairs office typing and pumping. She is a rock star. Same goes for my magnificent husband, who operates from a place of "my wife can do anything," and my light beam of a three-year-old, who couldn't care less what Mama's doing as long as there's snacks. They kept me uplifted and grounded.

I have to give major snaps to my agent Howard Yoon, my cheer-leader for more than a decade, who is always down for one more crazy idea. Also big thanks to Simone Hunter-Hobson, who helped research this book.

Thank you to everyone who told me their stories about Congresswoman Waters, a woman who leaves an indelible impression on everyone she comes into contact with, whether in person or one's own imagination, including this writer.

FROM ERIC

Perhaps it's gauche to acknowledge one's coauthor, but when you have the opportunity to work with Helena Andrews-Dyer—*especially* while she is, as she noted, immediately postpartum—it cannot go without mentioning. Helena, it's a privilege.

Thank you to my always-incredible agent Anna Sproul-Latimer, as well as the teams at Ross Yoon and Neon Literary.

My family at Elle.com encouraged my initial writing about Representative Waters and were enthusiastic cheerleaders about this project. I'm grateful to join you every day. Special thanks to Leah Chernikoff and Katie Connor for their leadership and vision.

As always, every word I write, every revision I stress over, every big idea with which I wrestle is shared with my brilliant husband, David Norse Thomas, and supported by my extraordinary parents, Bob and Judi Thomas. Thank you.

NOTES

INTRODUCTION

4 ***"I do say outrageous things sometimes":*** Interview by R. Eric Thomas with Maxine Waters, December 5, 2017.

4 ***the worst she's ever seen:*** *On One with Angela Rye,* podcast, July 12, 2017, https://soundcloud.com/ononewithangelarye/queen-maxine-feat-maxine -waters.

7 ***"too skinny" and "too black":*** Eleanor Clift and Tom Brazaitis, *War Without Bloodshed* (New York: Simon & Schuster, 1997), 267–68 (hereafter *War Without Bloodshed*).

CHAPTER ONE: THE MEME

11 ***"Is there some reason":*** "International Financial System," C-SPAN, July 27, 2017, https://www.c-span.org/video/?431675-1/treasury-secretary-testifies -state-international-finance-system.

13 ***"[Any] Member who has been recognized":*** Elizabeth Rybicki, "Speaking on the House Floor: Gaining Time and Parliamentary Phraseology," Congressional Research Service, December 10, 2018.

15 ***"The idea behind speaking":*** Interview by Helena Andrews-Dyer with Donald Garrett, December 2019.

16 ***"Yeah, that surprised me":*** K. K. Ottesen, "Maxine Waters: 'If I Want to Fight, I Want to Fight with the Lions,'" *The Washington Post Magazine,* August 27, 2019.

16 ***the Treasury secretary once again:*** Damian Paletta and Erica Werner, "Mnuchin, Waters Engage in Angry Exchange with Cameras Rolling on Capitol Hill," *Washington Post,* April 9, 2019.

17 ***"I have a foreign leader":*** "International Financial System," C-SPAN, July 27, 2017, https://www.c-span.org/video/?431675-1/treasury-secretary -testifies-state-international-finance-system.

18 ***"And I think that":*** Ottesen, "Maxine Waters."

CHAPTER TWO: MAXINE IN THE MAKING

22 **"[I was] the first in my family":** *War Without Bloodshed*, 267–68.

22 **a tiny Mississippi Delta town:** "Velma Lee Carr Moore," obituary, *St. Louis American*, 2014.

23 **"If my father was someone":** *War Without Bloodshed*, 268.

23 **"strong" and "survivor":** Marilyn Marshall, "America's Most Influential Black Woman Politician," *Ebony*, August 1994.

23 **"She did not raise us":** Taryn Finley, "Maxine Waters on the Strong Black Women Who Taught Her to Create Her Seat at the Table," *Huffington Post*, April 18, 2017.

23 **"who was going to wear":** Ibid.

24 **"She had no filters":** Janet Mock, "Auntie Maxine Waters Is Reading All Your Tweets," *Lenny Letter*, June 14, 2017 (hereafter *Lenny Letter*).

24 **"She was not an educated woman":** Maxine Waters, "Everyone Who Gave Us Life in 2017 Starring Maxine Waters," *Essence*, December 2017.

25 **"I think probably":** Maxine Waters, interview, Summit 21 Conference, Atlanta, Georgia, June 8, 2019.

25 **"Everybody had big families":** Maxine Waters, "Next Millennium Conference: Ending Domestic Violence; Closing: Maxine Waters," U.S. Department of Justice, September 27, 2000.

25 **"a little town":** *War Without Bloodshed*, 270.

26 **"I was never ashamed":** Douglas Shuit, "Waters Is a Fighter; Ask Any Assemblyman," *Los Angeles Times*, September 11, 1987.

26 **"I never felt helpless":** Finley, "Maxine Waters on the Strong Black Women Who Taught Her."

26 **"I have come to believe":** Joy Bennet Kinnon, "Ten Who Beat Welfare," *Ebony*, November 1996.

27 **"They were sad":** Waters, "Next Millennium Conference."

27 **"a very hardworking woman":** *War Without Bloodshed*, 271.

28 **"[My mother] didn't always understand":** Ibid.

28 **"Just getting heard":** Marshall, "America's Most Influential Black Woman Politician."

28 **"We had to scramble":** *War Without Bloodshed*, 270.

28 **almost every evening:** Jamia Wilson, "Maxine Waters Is Reclaiming Her Time," *Bust*, December/January 2017.

28 **"This is just amazing":** *War Without Bloodshed*, 271.

28 **They fed her:** Finley, "Maxine Waters on the Strong Black Women Who Taught Her."

29 ***"We had teachers":*** *War Without Bloodshed,* 270.

29 ***Louise Carter taught:*** Gordon F. Sander, "The Teacher Who Inspired Me," *Parade,* November 20, 1994.

29 ***"I would be left behind":*** Ibid.

29 ***"And it stayed with me":*** Ibid.

30 ***"Look at this":*** Marlo Thomas, *The Right Words at the Right Time* (New York: Atria Books, 2004), 368.

30 ***She wanted to be:*** Shonda Rhimes, "Rep. Maxine Waters Spills the Tea," *Shondaland,* September 17, 2017 (hereafter *Shondaland*).

30 ***"I also wanted":*** Ibid.

31 ***"They were perhaps":*** *War Without Bloodshed,* 273.

31 ***"always" worked, honey:*** Kinnon, "Ten Who Beat Welfare."

31 ***"We were all eager":*** *Lenny Letter.*

31 ***Maxine bused tables:*** Shuit, "Waters Is a Fighter."

32 ***The cafeteria's slogan:*** Michael Hauser and Marianne Weldon, *20th-Century Retailing in Downtown Grand Rapids* (Charleston, SC: Arcadia, 2014), 110.

32 ***"I just accepted it":*** Shuit, "Waters Is a Fighter."

32 ***"I think they saw Speaker":*** *War Without Bloodshed,* 271.

32 ***"It was a dead end":*** Interview by Helena Andrews-Dyer with Quincy Troupe, November 2019.

33 ***"Head Start changed my life":*** *War Without Bloodshed,* 272.

34 ***"It was exciting":*** Ronald Brownstein, "The Two Worlds of Maxine Waters: Mastering the Back Rooms of Sacramento, Battling Despair on the Streets of L.A.," *Los Angeles Times,* March 5, 1989.

34 ***"on two different tracks":*** *War Without Bloodshed,* 273.

TIME OUT: LIFE IN WATTS

35 ***"1,000 RIOT IN L.A.":*** *Los Angeles Times,* August 12, 1965.

35 ***By all accounts:*** "Marquette Frye, Whose Arrest Ignited the Watts Riots in 1965, Dies at Age 42," *Los Angeles Times,* December 25, 1986.

35 ***at least one officer's back:*** "Watts Riots, 40 Years Later," *Los Angeles Times,* August 11, 2005.

36 ***"Don't worry":*** "Marquette Frye, Whose Arrest Ignited the Watts Riots in 1965, Dies at Age 42."

36 ***"made enough money":*** "You're Black and That's All There Is to It," *Los Angeles Times,* October 10, 1965.

36 ***"I came from Mississippi":*** Ibid.

36 *"Whites have everything"*: Ibid.

37 *resulted in the deaths:* James Queally, "Watts Riots: Traffic Stop Was the Spark That Ignited Days of Destruction in L.A.," *Los Angeles Times,* July 29, 2015.

37 *She'd read the McCone Commission report:* "Jobs: Political Cure Lifts Few from Grip of Gang Life," *Los Angeles Times,* August 18, 1988.

37 *emergency literacy:* "25 Years After the Watts Riots: McCone Commission's Recommendations Have Gone Unheeded," *Los Angeles Times,* July 8, 1990.

38 *"To move families":* *Next Question with Katie Couric,* podcast, January 25, 2018.

38 *2 percentage points: Public Papers of the Presidents of the United States: Jimmy Carter,* 1979.

38 *a staggering 60 percent:* "Watts Remains a Powder Keg," *Eugene Register-Guard,* June 2, 1980.

38 *"black ribbon":* "Drive Against Police Brutality Launched by Woman Legislator," *Baltimore Afro-American,* June 10, 1980.

39 *1,500 unemployed people:* "Maxine Waters' 'Project Build': Job Training Program Goes Right to the Housing Projects for the People," *Los Angeles Times,* December 22, 1985.

39 *Waters pointed out:* "Jobs: Political Cure Lifts Few from Grip of Gang Life."

39 *"It's a struggle to say":* Ibid.

39 *"little SOBs":* Ibid.

39 *"There were several":* *Next Question with Katie Couric,* podcast, January 25, 2018.

40 *Attendees were instructed:* "Maxine Waters' 'Project Build': Job Training Program Goes Right to the Housing Projects for People."

40 *such luminaries as Jesse Jackson:* "Project Builds Where Hope Seems to Have Disappeared," *Los Angeles Times,* July 24, 1988.

40 *"We meet people":* Ibid.

40 *the lowest in the state:* Ibid.

40 *"The bureaucrats don't know":* Ibid.

41 *"People don't want to talk":* Brownstein, "The Two Worlds of Maxine Waters."

41 *"We have to learn":* "What They Said at the Summit," *Baltimore Afro-American,* April 29, 1989.

42 *"Do you think this 'pickaninny'":* "Constitution Panel Loses Funding over Skousen Text," *Deseret News,* March 5–8, 1987.

42 ***"Why should we trust you":*** Ibid.

43 ***"[at the Employment Center]":*** *Next Question with Katie Couric,* podcast, January 25, 2018.

43 ***"If you're black in America":*** "What They Said at the Summit."

THE TIMELINE

44 ***Senator Hiram Revels:*** "Black Americans in Congress: An Introduction," History, Art & Archives, U.S. House of Representatives, https://history .house.gov/Exhibitions-and-Publications/BAIC/Historical-Essays /Introduction/Introduction.

44 ***"Mr. Revels showed no embarrassment":*** "The Colored Member Admitted to His Seat in the Senate," *New York Times,* February 25, 1870.

45 ***Velma Lee, Maxine's mother:*** "Velma Lee Carr Moore."

45 ***"She** often **didn't":*** *War Without Bloodshed,* 271.

45 ***"I think they saw":*** Ibid.

45 ***the Head Start program:*** David Hudson, "This Day in History: The Creation of Head Start," WhiteHouse.gov, May 18, 2015, https://obamawhitehouse .archives.gov/blog/2015/05/18/day-history-creation-head-start.

45 ***Racial tensions explode:*** Queally, "Watts Riots: Traffic Stop Was the Spark."

46 ***"I discovered me":*** *War Without Bloodshed,* 272.

46 ***"what I really believed in":*** Brownstein, "The Two Worlds of Maxine Waters."

46 ***"All blacks are militant":*** Francis X. Clines, "Barbara Jordan Dies at 59; Her Voice Stirred the Nation," *New York Times,* January 18, 1996.

47 ***chief of staff to Councilman Cunningham:*** Carla Hall, "Sidney Williams' Unusual Route to Ambassador Post," *Los Angeles Times,* February 6, 1994.

47 ***"Jesse Jackson, thank you":*** Maxine Waters, "Honoring the 25th Anniversary of Jesse Jackson's Run for the Presidency," House floor speech, November 19, 2009, https://waters.house.gov/media-center/floor-statements/honoring -25th-anniversary-jesse-jacksons-run-presidency.

47 ***anti-apartheid divestment movement:*** Robert Lindsey, "California's Tough Line on Apartheid," *New York Times,* August 31, 1986.

48 ***"I don't intend":*** Maria Newman, "After the Riots: Washington at Work; Lawmaker from Riot Zone Insists on a New Role for Black Politicians," *New York Times,* May 19, 1992.

48 ***President George H. W. Bush:*** Sam Fulwood III, "Rep. Waters Labels Bush 'a Racist,' Endorses Clinton," *Los Angeles Times,* July 9, 1992.

48 ***"We are now":*** Catherine S. Manegold, "Sometimes the Order of the Day Is Just Maintaining Order," *New York Times,* July 30, 1994.

48 ***the Minority AIDS Initiative:*** Amy Goldstein, "U.S. to Begin Minority AIDS Initiative," *Washington Post,* October 29, 1998.

48 ***"call us unpatriotic":*** Maxine Waters, "War in Iraq," House floor speech, Iowa State University Archives of Women's Political Communication, March 18, 2002, https://awpc.cattcenter.iastate.edu/2017/03/21/war-in-iraq-march-18-2002.

49 ***"go straight to hell":*** Nia-Malika Henderson, "Maxine Waters to Tea Party: Go to Hell," *Washington Post,* August 22, 2011.

49 ***"has no credibility":*** Maxine Waters, Capitol Hill press conference, C-SPAN, January 13, 2017.

49 ***"stop his ass!":*** Vanessa Williams, "'Auntie Maxine' and the Quest for Impeachment," *Washington Post,* May 1, 2017.

49 ***"James Brown wig":*** Amy B. Wang, "Maxine Waters Swings Back at Bill O'Reilly: 'I'm a Strong Black Woman and I Cannot Be Intimidated,'" *Washington Post,* March 29, 2017.

49 ***O'Reilly is fired:*** Emily Steel and Michael S. Schmidt, "Bill O'Reilly Is Forced Out at Fox News," *New York Times,* April 19, 2017.

49 ***"I have the gavel":*** Emily Stewart, "'I Have the Gavel': Maxine Waters Lays Out an Aggressive Agenda at the House Financial Services Committee," Vox, January 16, 2019.

CHAPTER THREE: MS. WATERS GOES TO SACRAMENTO

52 ***"brought me in touch":*** *Lenny Letter.*

52 ***"There's only one way":*** James Richardson, *Willie Brown: A Biography* (Berkeley: University of California Press, 1998), 129.

53 ***"What I discovered":*** *War Without Bloodshed,* 272.

53 ***"She knew everybody":*** Interview by Helena Andres-Dyer with Raphael Sonenshein, November 2019. All quotes from Sonenshein in this chapter, unless otherwise noted, from this interview.

54 ***the highest-ranking black women:*** Raphael J. Sonenshein, *Politics in Black and White* (Princeton, NJ: Princeton University Press, 1993), 125.

54 ***"The thing about Maxine":*** Interview by Helena Andres-Dyer with Rick Taylor, December 2019.

54 ***"When Maxine spoke":*** Interview by Helena Andres-Dyer with Zev Yaroslavsky, November 2019. All quotes from Yaroslavsky in this chapter, unless otherwise noted, from this interview.

55 *"I couldn't keep doing both"*: Jocelyn Y. Stewart, "Leon D. Ralph, 74; Turned to the Ministry After Serving in State Assembly," *Los Angeles Times*, February 10, 2007.

55 *"When I arrived at the desk"*: Interview with Leon Ralph, California State Archive State Government Oral History Program, March 1990.

56 *"Something's wrong"*: *Lenny Letter*.

57 *"If Collins is the front runner"*: Narda Zacchino, "Democrats, Some with Political Ties, Battle in 48th Assembly District Race," *Los Angeles Times*, June 5, 1976.

58 *"I did move back"*: Ibid.

59 *"We had to figure out"*: *Shondaland*.

60 *"Is she a . . . [n-word]?"*: Ibid.

60 *the two-party vote:* Sonenshein, *Politics in Black and White*.

60 *"We had our whites"*: *Lenny Letter*.

60 *"For me to identify myself"*: Interview by Gloria Steinem with Maxine Waters, Sixth and I, Washington, D.C., October 28, 2015.

60 *"all of those women"*: *Shondaland*.

60 *Mary B. Henry:* Carol J. Williams, "Mary B. Henry Dies at 82; Civil Rights Activist Improved Education, Healthcare in L.A.," *Los Angeles Times*, August 16, 2009.

60 *Opal Jones:* Annelise Orleck and Lisa Gayle Hazirjian, *The War on Poverty: A New Grassroots History* (Athens: University of Georgia Press, 2011), 212.

61 *Lillian Harkless Mobley:* Jocelyn Y. Stewart, "Lillian Mobley Dies at 81; South Los Angeles Activist," *Los Angeles Times*, July 21, 2011.

61 *"I met wonderful women"*: *Shondaland*.

61 *"perhaps the biggest upset"*: Larry Stammer, "Incumbent Legislators, Women Have Field Day," *Los Angeles Times*, June 10, 1976.

61 *"It's really a simple"*: Ibid.

61 *The room was so shocked:* War Without Bloodshed, 275.

61 *"Men attacked me"*: Diane Seo, "Reigning Women: 'Year of the Woman'? In Central L.A. They've Wielded Political Clout for Years—and More Are on the Way," *Los Angeles Times*, November 29, 1992.

TIME OUT: THE NATIONAL WOMEN'S CONFERENCE OF 1977

62 *"Madame Chairperson, I am"*: Christi Collier, National Women's Conference: A Question of Choices, KERA-TV, 1977 (hereafter A Question of Choices).

62 **"It was a constitutional convention":** Gloria Steinem, *My Life on the Road* (New York: Random House, 2016), 54.

63 **"the invisible women":** Caroline Bird, *The Spirit of Houston: The First National Women's Conference, Official Report to the President, the Congress and the People of the United States,* March 1978 (hereafter *Spirit of Houston*).

63 **"writing down concerns":** Steinem, *My Life on the Road,* 60.

63 **"clear, strong voice":** *Spirit of Houston,* 158.

63 **"The noisy floor":** Ibid.

64 **"The united minority caucus":** A Question of Choices.

65 **"on behalf of the black women":** Ibid.

65 **"Let this message go forth":** Steinem, *My Life on the Road,* 157.

CHAPTER FOUR: INTERNATIONAL IMPLICATIONS

68 *tuned a little radio:* "Blacks Sit In to Protest Apartheid," *Los Angeles Times,* January 4, 1985.

68 *she'd start her days:* "Local Elections 29th Congressional District," *Los Angeles Times,* May 29, 1985.

69 *24 million black South Africans:* "Blacks Sit In to Protest Apartheid."

69 *72 percent of the nation's population:* "Consequences for U.S. Cited: Tutu Pleads for Help in Heading Off a Racial War," *Los Angeles Times,* May 14, 1985.

69 **"most oppressed, racist nation":** "Panel Votes to End State Pension Links to S. Africa," *Los Angeles Times,* April 30, 1985.

70 *could not get a single vote:* Lindsey, "California's Tough Line on Apartheid."

70 *Waters was joined:* "Blacks Sit In to Protest Apartheid."

71 **"a continued escalation":** Ibid.

71 **"for goodness' sake":** "Consequences for U.S. Cited: Tutu Pleads for Help in Heading Off a Racial War."

71 *begun as early as 1973:* "Faculty Rallies with Students on Apartheid," *Deseret News,* April 18–19, 1985.

72 *political pressure, diplomatic pressure:* "Consequences for U.S. Cited: Tutu Pleads for Help in Heading Off a Racial War."

72 *UC Berkeley alone:* Figures quoted in "Panel Votes to End State Pension Links to S. Africa."

72 *Berkeley stood to lose $100 million:* "Debate on S. Africa Stalls State Budget Compromise," *Los Angeles Times,* June 8, 1985.

72 **"The dollars of any American firm":** "Divestiture Bill's Cost Put at $50 Million."

73 ***"It is so important"***: "Faculty Rallies with Students on Apartheid."

74 ***"My personal opinion"***: "Debate on S. Africa Stalls State Budget Compromise."

74 ***provided military supplies:*** "Divestiture Plan Approved: Compromise Clears Way for State Budget OK," *Los Angeles Times,* June 12, 1985.

75 ***"I have concluded"***: "Deukmejian Keeps Ban on Funds for Abortion Groups: OKs Record Budget of $34.8 Billion," *Los Angeles Times,* June 28, 1985.

76 ***"key" to the bill's passage:*** "Divestiture Bill's Cost Put at $50 Million."

76 ***"That moved me to say no"***: *Next Question with Katie Couric,* podcast, January 18, 2018.

76 ***didn't go far enough:*** "Governor Will Veto Measure on Apartheid," *Los Angeles Times,* September 13, 1985.

76 ***"It simply requests"***: "Governor Offers Substitute Plan on S. Africa Funds," *Los Angeles Times,* September 19, 1985.

77 ***"I think it's very relevant"***: "Governor Will Veto Measure on Apartheid."

77 ***He was trying:*** "With Lobbies in Full Cry, California Debates Repealing Multinational Tax," *New York Times,* February 18, 1986.

77 ***$12.3 million in stock:*** "Students Favor Divestment but Shun Boycott of Products: Scope of S. Africa Protests Questioned," *Los Angeles Times,* April 16, 1986.

78 ***"California cannot ignore"***: "Governor Shifts Stand, Calls for Full Divestiture," *Los Angeles Times,* July 17, 1986.

78 ***"I think a lot of it"***: Lindsey, "California's Tough Line on Apartheid."

78 ***It was larger:*** "California Senate Passes Bill to Sell Pretoria-Linked Stock," *New York Times,* August 26, 1986.

78 ***"The state of California"***: "Governor Gets Landmark Bill on Divestiture," *Los Angeles Times,* August 28, 1986.

TIME OUT: MAXINE AND SIDNEY

79 ***"She talked about how"***: Interview by Helena Andrews-Dyer with Rick Taylor.

79 ***"I have my career"***: Aldore Collier, "A Black Woman's Place Is in the . . . House of Representatives," *Ebony,* January 1991.

CHAPTER FIVE: UPRISING

82 ***Waters had long been:*** Brownstein, "The Two Worlds of Maxine Waters."

82 *his heir apparent:* "Rep. Hawkins Says He Won't Run Again; Waters to Seek Seat," *Los Angeles Times,* January 27, 1990.

82 *"the charismatic kind":* Ibid.

83 *"There are no obvious ones":* Ibid.

83 *"America's Most Influential":* Marshall, "The Most Influential Black Woman Politician."

83 *the tune of $40,000:* "Local Elections 29th Congressional District," *Los Angeles Times,* May 29, 1990.

84 *to gain "intelligence":* Ibid.

84 *the number of ballots:* "Final California Election Results: Congressional Races," *Los Angeles Times,* November 8, 1990.

84 *"I'm going to do":* "California Elections/Congress: No Surprises in Voting: Incumbents Win Easily," *Los Angeles Times,* November 8, 1990.

84 *"We're not jumping":* Brownstein, "The Two Worlds of Maxine Waters."

85 *the officers would later claim:* "Taped 'Sting' Shows Police Clash with Black in Arrest," *Los Angeles Times,* January 16, 1989.

85 *What it did show:* Ibid.

86 *would later call an epidemic:* "U.S. Inquiry Sought in Police Beating," *New York Times,* March 13, 1991.

86 *a breaking point:* "One Ex-Cop's Quest to Uncover Racist Officers," Associated Press, May 27, 1997.

86 *"hypersensitive to racism":* Ibid.

86 *his litmus test:* "Officer Hits the Prime Time with Video Camera," *Los Angeles Times,* January 20, 1989.

86 *he'd stopped to witness:* Ibid.

87 *four-hundred-year-old:* "One Ex-Cop's Quest to Uncover Racist Officers."

87 *"You can't bait":* "Officer Hits the Prime Time with Video Camera."

87 *a provocative ambush:* "Violence Is the Best-Kept Police Secret," *Los Angeles Times,* January 27, 1989.

87 *"No one ever documented":* "A Private Mod Squad Sets Out to Prove Police Harassment—and Stirs a Fight Over Its Tactics," *People,* December 11, 1989.

88 *"a faulty memory":* "Officer Admits He Erred in Report on Videotaped Arrest," *Los Angeles Times,* March 4, 1989.

88 *"When it happened":* *Next Question with Katie Couric,* podcast, January 25, 2018.

88 *"Oh my god!":* "Maxine Waters: '92 L.A. Rebellion Was a 'Defining Moment' for Black Resistance," *Huffington Post,* April 27, 2017.

89 ***"a bit of action":*** "Cameraman's Test Puts Him in the Spotlight," *Los Angeles Times,* March 7, 1991.

89 ***King had been Tasered:*** *Report of the Independent Commission on the Los Angeles Police Department,* 1991, https://web.archive.org/web/20110 722124708/http:/www.parc.info/client_files/Special%20Reports/1%20 -%20Chistopher%20Commision.pdf.

89 ***"Gorillas in the Mist":*** Ibid., 71.

89 ***"Deft recovered":*** Ibid., 9.

89 ***"the greatest single barrier":*** Ibid., xx.

90 ***The desk officer:*** Ibid., 46.

90 ***a fractured eye socket:*** "Los Angeles Jury Widens Inquiry in Police Beating," *New York Times,* March 10, 1991.

90 ***They purchased the footage:*** "Cameraman's Test Puts Him in the Spotlight."

90 ***"an aberration":*** "U.S. Inquiry Sought in Police Beating."

90 ***"This is the order":*** Ibid.

90 ***a poll conducted:*** *Report of the Independent Commission on the Los Angeles Police Department,* 1991, https://web.archive.org/web/20110722124708 /http://www.parc.info/client_files/Special%20Reports/1%20-%20 Chistopher%20Commision.pdf, 16.

90 ***"It is apparent":*** Ibid., 9.

90 ***"He's on parole":*** "Gates Offers an Apology," *Los Angeles Times,* March 9, 1991.

91 ***they locked the doors:*** "How the Deal Was Struck on Gates' Retirement Date," *Los Angeles Times,* July 24, 1991.

92 ***"a Watts revolution":*** "Rampage in Westwood," *Los Angeles Times,* March 10, 1991.

92 ***more than one hundred:*** "Gates Provides Details About Fatal Shooting of Watts Man by Police," *Los Angeles Times,* December 13, 1991.

92 ***"The people there":*** "Waters Calls for Probe of Shooting: Police: She Says L.A. Is 'on Verge of Holocaust' after LAPD Slaying of Man at Watts Housing Project," *Los Angeles Times,* December 18, 1991.

92 ***"make sure the police":*** "Waters Pledges Help at Imperial Courts," *Los Angeles Times,* January 1, 1992.

93 ***"The police grabbed me":*** "Residents Complain of Abuse by Police," *Los Angeles Times,* January 15, 1992.

93 ***six hours of deliberation:*** "All 4 Acquitted in King Beating," *Los Angeles Times,* April 30, 1992.

94 *decrying "lawlessness":* "Bush Denounces Rioting in L.A. as 'Purely Criminal,'" *Los Angeles Times,* May 1, 1992.

94 *"a cancer of racism":* Ibid.

94 *"We simply cannot condone":* Ibid.

94 *"Let's be straight":* "Maxine Waters Reacts to Acquittal of Officers Who Beat Rodney King," https://www.youtube.com/watch?v=WNNtUriT96E.

95 *"I'm very pained":* "'Cosby' Finale: Not All Drama Was in the Streets," *Los Angeles Times,* May 2, 1992.

97 *"because they are not":* "Clinton Issues Plea for Racial Harmony," *Washington Post,* May 3, 1992.

98 *"I'd get up early":* "Maxine Waters: '92 L.A. Rebellion Was a 'Defining Moment' for Black Resistance."

98 *"What did you expect?":* "How Do You Explain the King Case to a 9-Year-Old?" *Los Angeles Times,* May 4, 1992.

98 *"just one of the victims":* "Waters Focuses Her Rage at System: Politics: She Says Inner-City Woes Have Been Simmering and Need Action," *Los Angeles Times,* May 10, 1992.

99 *Waters urged leaders:* "No Insurrection in Los Angeles," *Washington Post,* May 4, 1992.

99 *"There are those":* "Maxine Waters Reacts to Acquittal of Officers Who Beat Rodney King," https://www.youtube.com/watch?v=WNNtUriT96E.

99 *"I Know How to Talk":* Anna Deavere Smith, *Twilight: Los Angeles, 1992* (New York: Dramatists Play Service, 2003), 162.

100 *"This Rodney King":* "California Commentary: 'Through It . . .' by Maxine Waters," *Los Angeles Times,* April 14, 1993.

100 *"Each day brings":* Ibid.

100 *"We have got to live!":* Ibid.

TIME OUT: THE PRESIDENTS

101 *"I don't ever want":* "Black Elected Officials Take Notice," *Afro-American,* May 23, 1992.

103 *Included on that list:* "Jackson Offers Mondale Black Women Candidates," *Deseret News,* July 3, 1984.

103 *"I don't have time":* "AKA & Jack & Jill Conventions," *Afro-American,* August 4, 1984.

104 *"The federal government's failure":* "Bush Offers Message of Healing to the City," *Los Angeles Times,* May 8, 1992.

104 ***"I can't over-promise":*** "President Tours L.A. Riot Zone, Asks for Advice; 'Please Speak Frankly,'" *Baltimore Sun,* May 8, 1992.

104 ***a day late:*** "Bush Offers Message of Healing to the City."

104 ***"How many more rebellions":*** Ibid.

104 ***"I don't intend":*** Newman, "After the Riots."

105 ***"a mean-spirited man":*** Fulwood, "Rep. Waters Labels Bush 'a Racist,' Endorses Clinton."

106 ***"George Bush a racist":*** "Quayle Demands Clinton Apologize for Waters' Attack on Bush," *Los Angeles Times,* August 7, 1992.

106 ***"wants an apology":*** Ibid.

106 ***"Dan Quayle doesn't know me":*** "Waters: No Apologies for Her Calling the President a Racist," *Los Angeles Times,* August 9, 1992.

106 ***"He is the epitome":*** "Political Forecast: Will Quayle Be on the '92 Ticket or Playing Golf?" *Los Angeles Times,* May 12, 1991.

107 ***"This is the last time":*** "Waters Keeps Walking a Fine Line with Clinton," *Los Angeles Times,* July 16, 1992.

107 ***She knew that:*** "*Los Angeles Times* Interview: Maxine Waters: Veteran Legislator Makes People Angry—but She's Never Ignored," *Los Angeles Times,* May 16, 1993.

107 ***30 percent of black voters:*** "Black Voters Remain Cautious About Clinton," *Los Angeles Times,* July 13, 1992.

108 ***"in its attempts to get":*** Ibid.

108 ***"Let me tell you":*** "'92 Democratic Convention," *Los Angeles Times,* July 16, 1992.

108 ***for HUD secretary:*** "*Los Angeles Times* Interview: Maxine Waters: Veteran Legislator Makes People Angry—but She's Never Ignored."

108 ***his approval rating:*** "Presidential Approval Ratings—Bill Clinton," Gallup, https://news.gallup.com/poll/116584/presidential-approval-ratings-bill -clinton.aspx.

108 ***"I really do believe":*** "*Los Angeles Times* Interview: Maxine Waters: Veteran Legislator Makes People Angry—but She's Never Ignored."

109 ***"I will not be healed":*** ". . . But Can He Handle the Job?" *Wilmington Morning Star,* December 26, 2000.

109 ***"Ashcroft represents everything":*** "Gaining, and Losing, Too," *New York Times,* February 2, 2001.

109 ***"reining in this president":*** "U.S. House Begins Full Debate on the Iraq War," *New York Times,* February 14, 2007.

110 ***Excerpt from Floor Statement:*** "The Iraq War," August 4, 2009, https://waters.house.gov/media-center/floor-statemements/iraq-war.

112 ***"We don't put pressure":*** "Rep. Waters to Black Voters: 'Unleash Us' on Obama," TheGrio, August 17, 2011.

112 ***"We should be in front":*** Ibid.

112 ***"We love the president":*** Maxine Waters, interview, CNN, August 19, 2011.

113 ***"So I don't know":*** "Remarks by the President at Congressional Black Caucus Foundation Annual Phoenix Awards Dinner," Washington Convention Center, Washington, D.C., September 24, 2011, https://obamawhitehouse.archives.gov/the-press-office/2016/09/18/remarks-president-congressional-black-caucus-foundation-46th-annual.

113 ***"I don't know who":*** Maxine Waters, interview, *CBS Early Show,* September 2011.

113 ***"Many of those people":*** Maxine Waters, interview, CNN, September 2011.

113 ***"But I certainly don't":*** Maxine Waters, interview, MSNBC, September 2011.

CHAPTER SIX: SHUT UP

118 ***In the C-SPAN video:*** "Whitewater Controversy Clip," C-SPAN, July 29, 1994, https://www.c-span.org/video/?59124-1/whitewater-controversy-clip.

120 ***King came out swinging:*** "Whitewater Controversy on House Floor," C-SPAN, July 29, 1994, https://www.c-span.org/video/?59115-1/whitewater-controversy-house-floor.

122 ***"[King] had to be":*** Ibid.

124 ***so she assumed:*** "Waters-King Verbal Slugfest Spills Over onto House Floor," *Los Angeles Times,* July 30, 1994.

125 ***"People are not accustomed":*** Real Clear Politics, October 24, 2017, https://www.realclearpolitics.com/video/2017/10/24/maxine_waters_trump_supporters_not_accustomed_to_a_black_woman_taking_leadership_to_impeach_him.html.

126 ***"a very aggressive":*** Shuit, "Waters Is a Fighter; Ask Any Assemblyman."

126 ***"I am sick and tired":*** "Telling It Like It Is in L.A.," *Ebony,* October 1992, 35.

127 ***"Those who consider themselves":*** Shuit, "Waters Is a Fighter; Ask Any Assemblyman."

CHAPTER SEVEN: WALL STREET AND GANGSTERS

130 *Maxine Waters's favorite rapper: On One with Angela Rye,* podcast, July 11, 2017, https://soundcloud.com/ononewithangelarye/queen-maxine-feat -maxine-waters.

131 *"Don't these politicians realize":* "The Uncivil War: The Battle Between the Establishment and Supporters of Rap Music Reopens Old Wounds of Race and Class," *Los Angeles Times,* July 19, 1992.

132 *"The reason why rap":* Ibid.

132 *rap music had become:* Ibid.

132 *"While I find some":* "Rap Finds a Supporter in Rep. Maxine Waters," *Los Angeles Times,* February 15, 1994.

133 *the 435-member House:* 102nd Congress figures: Congressional Research Service, *Representatives and Senators: Trends in Member Characteristics Since 1945,* February 2012, https://fas.org/sgp/crs/misc/R42365.pdf; 103rd Congress figures: "New Voices Shake Up the House," *Los Angeles Times,* July 5, 1993.

133 *The House was bigger: On One with Angela Rye,* podcast, July 11, 2017, https://soundcloud.com/ononewithangelarye/queen-maxine-feat-maxine -waters.

134 *get off the committee:* Ibid.

134 *"that banking committee":* Ibid.

134 *"Well, I know that some people": The Breakfast Club,* August 7, 2017, https://www.youtube.com/watch?v=6D5Wkw95xtE&feature=emb_title (hereafter *The Breakfast Club*).

135 *"Billions is what is spent":* "Maxine Waters: Veteran Legislator Makes People Angry—but She's Never Ignored."

135 *Banking, she thought:* "Telling It Like It Is in L.A.," 35.

135 *"Whether we're talking":* Ibid.

136 *"These are the gangsters": The Breakfast Club.*

136 *"the first former welfare mother":* "Congresswoman Lynn Woolsey: Biography," archived at https://web.archive.org/web/20120210101207 /http://woolsey.house.gov/index.cfm?sectionid=31&sectiontree=2%2C31.

137 *"I was lucky":* "Defying Poverty: Former Welfare Mother Tells Her Story in Campaign," *Los Angeles Times,* October 17, 1992.

137 *"[With the release]": On One with Angela Rye,* podcast, July 11, 2017, https://soundcloud.com/ononewithangelarye/queen-maxine-feat-maxine -waters.

138 *"I thought it was creative":* The Breakfast Club.

138 *"Creativity, we've always seen":* "Afeni Shakur, Survivor," *XXL,* October 2003, https://www.xxlmag.com/news/2012/09/afeni-shakur-survivor-story-from-xxls-october-2003-issue.

139 *"Tupac, for me":* On One with Angela Rye, podcast, July 11, 2017, https://soundcloud.com/ononewithangelarye/queen-maxine-feat-maxine-waters.

139 *"Look on a street corner":* "Maxine Waters: Hard Cases Hold the Key to Urban Peace," *Los Angeles Times,* June 13, 1993.

140 *"The great enemies":* "Rep. Waters Wins $50 Million for Urban Youth," *Jet,* July 26, 1993, 57.

141 *"Rap will likely":* "Rap; Still in Its Adolescence," *New York Times,* March 27, 1994.

141 *"It gives [rappers] a sense":* "Hard-Core Rap Lyrics Stir Backlash," *New York Times,* August 15, 1993.

141 *"It would be a foolhardy mistake":* "Rap Finds a Supporter in Rep. Maxine Waters."

141 *"We have declared war":* Ibid.

142 *"I personally am hurt":* Subcommittee on Juvenile Justice, Committee of the Judiciary, *Shaping Our Responses to Violent and Demeaning Imagery in Popular Music,* 103rd Cong., 2nd sess., 1994, 86.

142 *"These are my children":* Ibid., 7.

142 *"For the past three years":* Ibid., 9.

143 *"You have sold your souls":* "Dole Campaign Speech," C-SPAN, May 31, 1995, https://www.c-span.org/video/?65642-1/dole-campaign-speech.

143 *"This is not about parties":* "Lyrics from the Gutter," *New York Times,* June 2, 1995.

143 *"Some rappers want to put":* "Generation Rap," *New York Times,* April 3, 1994.

144 *"Some people would like":* "Rap Finds a Supporter in Rep. Maxine Waters."

144 *"there was no other platform":* Ibid.

TIME OUT: THE WORK

146 *the average number:* "Table 6-1 House Workload, 80th–113th Congresses, 1947–2014," Brookings Institution, https://www.brookings.edu/wp-content/uploads/2017/01/vitalstats_ch6_tbl1.pdf.

148 *Waters said, "I authored":* "President Obama Signs Haiti Debt Relief Bill Authored by Congresswoman Waters into Law," https://waters.house.gov /media-center/press-releases/president-obama-signs-haiti-debt-relief-bill -authored-congresswoman.

148 *"This legislation addresses":* "House Passes Congresswoman Waters' Flood Insurance Bill," https://waters.house.gov/media-center/press-releases /house-passes-congresswoman-waters-flood-insurance-bill.

149 *By the Numbers:* "Representative Maxine Waters," Congress.gov, https:// www.congress.gov/member/maxine-waters/W000187?searchResultView Type=expanded&KWICView=false.

CHAPTER EIGHT: THERE ARE LOWS TO THIS

152 *who pushed Obama:* Michael Finnegan and Janet Hook, "Trickle of Superdelegates Turns to Surge for Obama," *Los Angeles Times,* June 4, 2008.

153 *"Why is it that":* Maxine Waters, press conference, Capitol Visitors Center, August 13, 2010 (hereafter Waters Press Conference).

153 *"some people in town":* Report and Findings, Office of Congressional Ethics, August 6, 2009 (hereafter Ethics Report).

153 *"The system has not":* Waters Press Conference.

155 *Frank advised Waters:* Ethics Report.

155 *"had zero impact":* Susan Schmidt, "Waters Helped Bank Whose Stock She Once Owned," *Wall Street Journal,* March 12, 2009.

156 *"I won't go behind":* Waters Press Conference.

156 *"I want to be absolutely clear":* Ibid.

157 *Mikael Moore, Maxine's grandson:* Lisa Mascaro, "Working for Grandma Waters on Capitol Hill," *Los Angeles Times,* August 12, 2010.

157 *"This is what I do":* Waters Press Conference.

158 *Tyler Perry-level:* R. Jeffrey Smith and Carol D. Leonnig, "Ethics Probe of Rep. Waters Derailed by Infighting, Sources Say," *Washington Post,* December 16, 2010.

158 *lawyer Billy Martin:* Carol D. Leonnig, "Maxine Waters's Case Punted to Outside Counsel," *Washington Post,* August 9, 2011.

158 *drop all charges:* Richard Simon, "House Ethics Committee Ends Maxine Waters Investigation," *Los Angeles Times,* September 25, 2012.

158 *"a letter of reproval":* John Bresnahan, "Waters Ethics Case Debacle Detailed," *Politico,* September 26, 2012.

159 ***"On any normal day":*** Interview by Helena Andrews with Sean Bartlett, December 2019.

159 ***"This is what I do":*** Joseph Williams, "Obama Learns Perils of Roiling Waters," *Politico,* October 20, 2011.

CHAPTER NINE: SHE BETTA WERK

162 ***"I don't honor him":*** Maxine Waters, interview, MSNBC, January 17, 2016.

162 ***"He's a liar!":*** Williams, " 'Auntie Maxine' and the Quest for Impeachment."

162 ***"Reclaiming my time":*** Maxine Waters, House Financial Services Committee hearing, July 27, 2017.

162 ***"She was so fly":*** Interview by Helena Andrews-Dyer with Michaela Angela Davis, November 2019. All quotes from Davis in this chapter are from this interview.

162 ***"being a fearless":*** Mesfin Fekadu, "Rep. Maxine Waters to Be Honored at BET's Black Girls Rock," Associated Press, August 3, 2017.

163 ***"I want you to know":*** Maxine Waters, *Black Girls Rock! 2017,* BET Network, August 5, 2017.

165 ***"In this era of smooth":*** Brownstein, "The Two Worlds of Maxine Waters."

165 ***"She's very chic":*** Interview by Helena Andrews-Dyer with Teri Agins, November 2019. All quotes from Agins in this chapter are from this interview.

167 ***"how you dressed":*** Interview by Helena Andrews-Dyer with Robin Givhan, November 2019. All quotes from Givhan in this chapter are from this interview.

168 ***"I would get terrible grades":*** *War Without Bloodshed,* 269.

168 ***"I love clothes":*** Ibid.

169 ***settling sexual harassment:*** Paul Farhi, "Report: Bill O'Reilly Settled Sexual Harassment Claim from Fox News Contributor for $32 Million," *Washington Post,* October 21, 2017.

169 ***"When we fight against":*** Maxine Waters, House floor speech, C-SPAN, March 27, 2017.

169 ***"I didn't hear a word":*** Bill O'Reilly, *Fox and Friends,* Fox News, March 28, 2017.

170 ***"nappy-headed hoes":*** Robert Smith, "CBS Fires Don Imus in Fallout over Remarks," NPR, April 12, 2017.

170 ***"Let me just say this":*** Maxine Waters, *All In with Chris Hayes,* MSNBC, March 28, 2017.

TIME OUT: AND NOW A WORD FROM THE BOOK OF MAXINE

173 *"She's been called 'Kerosene Maxine'":* "Maxine Waters a Model for Many Outspoken Freshman Democrats," Associated Press, May 8, 2019.

173 *"I think it was born":* "Maxine Waters Is Learning from Millennials," *The New York Times Magazine,* July 19, 2017.

174 *"I am an experienced legislator":* Interview by R. Eric Thomas with Maxine Waters, December 5, 2017.

175 *"I've got it made":* "Local Elections: Congress: Maxine Waters Already Is Staking Out Her Claim," *Los Angeles Times,* October 1, 1990.

175 *"I think she's going":* "Maxine Waters Already Is Staking Out Her Claim," *Los Angeles Times,* October 1, 1990.

176 *"As an African American woman":* The Breakfast Club.

178 *"You got the first":* "Biden's Description of Obama Draws Scrutiny," CNN, February 9, 2007, https://www.cnn.com/2007/POLITICS/01/31 /biden.obama.

178 *"Biden's comments":* Ibid.

179 *"The image of being tough":* Brownstein, "The Two Worlds of Maxine Waters."

182 *"I'm absolutely determined":* Interview by R. Eric Thomas with Maxine Waters, December 5, 2017.

183 *"I am an experienced legislator":* Ibid.

184 *someone who won their election:* Virginia House of Delegates member Shelly Simonds beat David Yancey by one vote in a recount in December 2017.

CHAPTER TEN: "I'M NOT AFRAID OF ANYBODY"

188 *"I would not waste my time":* "Maxine Waters Is Learning from Millennials."

189 *Maxine Waters is not afraid:* "Rep. Maxine Waters Says 'The Tea Party Can Go Straight to Hell,'" CBSNews.com, August 22, 2011, https://www .cbsnews.com/news/rep-maxine-waters-says-tea-party-can-go-straight-to -hell.

189 *the "whitelash":* "After Calling Their Votes a 'Whitelash' Van Jones Finds a New Role Reaching Out to Trump Supporters," *Washington Post,* March 20, 2017.

190 *A 2010 survey:* "Are Tea Partiers Racist?" *Newsweek,* April 25, 2010.

190 *A New York Times/CBS News poll:* "Poll Finds Tea Party Backers Wealthier and More Educated," *New York Times,* April 14, 2010.

190 *"The president is going"*: "Rep. Maxine Waters Says 'The Tea Party Can Go Straight to Hell.'"

190 *"I'm not afraid of"*: "Video: Democrat Maxine Waters Tells the Tea Party to Go to Hell," FoxNews.com, August 22, 2011, https://video.foxnews.com/v/1122611179001#sp=show-clips.

191 *"And as far as I'm"*: "Rep. Maxine Waters Says 'The Tea Party Can Go Straight to Hell.'"

191 *"And I intend"*: "Video: Democrat Maxine Waters Tells the Tea Party to Go to Hell."

193 *"whether or not you will defend"*: *On One with Angela Rye*, podcast, July 12, 2017, https://soundcloud.com/ononewithangelarye/queen-maxine-feat-maxine-waters.

195 *"You know what?"*: "'Auntie Maxine' Waters Goes After Trump and Goes Viral," *New York Times*, July 7, 2017.

196 *a "disgusting, poor excuse"*: Ibid.

196 *"Impeachment is not good enough"*: Tweet from @RepMaxineWaters, October 1, 2019, https://twitter.com/RepMaxineWaters/status/1179083422712700928.

196 *"He's embarrassing us"*: "Maxine Waters on Trump: He Doesn't Even Know How to Spell His Wife's Name," *San Francisco Chronicle*, July 14, 2018.

196 *"I think he believes in nothing"*: *The Breakfast Club*.

197 *"Ladies and gentlemen"*: "Watch: Rep. Waters Says Impeachment Vote 'Was Not Inevitable, but It Was Predictable,'" https://www.youtube.com/watch?v=iZdbMNNJcik.

CHAPTER ELEVEN: FINAL THOUGHTS

203 *"You're so wonderful!"*: Tweet from @RepMaxineWaters, July 31, 2017, https://twitter.com/RepMaxineWaters/status/892197204278083585.

APPENDIX: MAXINE IN THE MEDIA

207 *"Reclaiming My Time"*: "Reclaiming My Time: Gospel Remix," lyrics reprinted with the permission of Mykal Kilgore.

CREDITS

INTRODUCTION

Waters holds a shirt with her image and catchphrase made by Nineteenth Amendment clothing: The 19th DC Democrat Fashion (www.the19thdc.com)

Waters in 2017: Photograph by Chelsea Guglielmino/Getty Images

CHAPTER ONE

Waters in 2019: Photograph by Chip Somodevilla/Getty Images

Three-year-old Arya George dresses as Representative Waters for Halloween: Photograph courtesy Sareena Davis and Ta-Leya Harris

TIME OUT: LIFE IN WATTS

Emancipation Proclamation (del., lith. and print. by L. Lipman, Milwaukee, Wisconsin): Library of Congress Prints and Photographs Division, LC-DIG-pga-02040

Senator Hiram R. Revels of Mississippi: Brady-Handy photograph collection, Library of Congress Prints and Photographs Division, LC-DIG-cwpbh-00554

Poster for presidential candidate Shirley Chisholm, 1972: Collection of the Smithsonian National Museum of African American History and Culture, Gifted with pride from Ellen Brooks.

Keynote address by Representative Barbara Jordan, Democratic National Convention, July 12, 1976: Photograph by Warren K. Leffler, Library of Congress Prints and Photographs Division, LC-U9-32937-32A/33

Pin-back button for women's equality: Collection of the Smithsonian National Museum of African American History and Culture, Gift of Family of Sarah Elizabeth Wright

Placard from March on Washington, August 28, 1963: Collection of the Smithsonian National Museum of African American History and Culture, Gift of Samuel Y. Edgerton Jr.

CHAPTER FOUR
Waters in her office in the California State Assembly in 1987: Photograph by Bob Riha, Jr./Getty Images

TIME OUT: MAXINE AND SIDNEY
Maxine Waters and Sidney Williams: Photograph by John Sciulli/Getty Images for NAACP Image Awards

CHAPTER FIVE
Maxine Waters's first election for Congress: Photograph by CQ Roll Call via AP Images

Waters outside the U.S. Capitol, 1995: Photograph by Anthony Barboza/Getty Images

Waters and President Bill Clinton tour South Central Los Angeles on May 4, 1992: Photograph by Jean-Marc Giboux/Getty Images

TIME OUT: THE PRESIDENTS
Waters and Jesse Jackson go way back. Here they sit side by side in 1984: Photograph by Jacques M. Chenet/CORBIS/Corbis via Getty Images

Waters speaks at the 1992 Democratic National Convention: Photograph by Jacques M. Chenet/CORBIS/Corbis via Getty Images

CHAPTER SIX
Waters in 1994: Photograph by Maureen Keating/CQ Roll Call via Getty Images

The Mace: Harris & Ewing Collection, Library of Congress Prints and Photographs Division, LC-DIG-hec-05553

Waters in February 1991: Photograph by Laura Patterson/CQ Roll Call via Getty Images

CHAPTER SEVEN
T.I. hugs Waters at the Forty-Seventh Annual CBC Legislative Conference: Photograph courtesy of Naaman Brown

TIME OUT: THE WORK
Waters and Representative Barney Frank, former chair of the House Financial Services Committee, make calls in 1998: Photograph by Karin Cooper/Getty Images

Waters in 1998, during a House Judiciary Committee hearing: Photograph by Rebecca Roth, Library of Congress Prints and Photographs Division, LC-DIG-ppmsca-38857

CHAPTER EIGHT
Waters confers with staff member in 2011: © 2011, Melina Mara/*Washington Post*

CHAPTER NINE
Waters strikes a pose at 2017's Black Girls Rock!: Photograph by Paul Zimmerman/WireImage

Waters in stripes in 2019: Photograph by Tom Williams/CQ Roll Call

Waters attends the 2019 California Democratic Party State Convention: Photograph by Gage Skidmore

Waters speaks at the 2016 Democratic National Convention in Philadelphia: © Michael Robinson Chavez/*Washington Post*

An exultant Waters at a 2017 Prayer Breakfast in Washington, D.C.: Photograph by Earl Gibson III/WireImage

TIME OUT: AND NOW A WORD FROM THE BOOK OF MAXINE
A now-iconic image of Waters listening during testimony in 2013: Photograph by Alex Wong/Getty Images

Waters, with Jesse Jackson, speaks at a Los Angeles Board of Supervisors hearing in 2004: Photograph by Robert Gauthier/*Los Angeles Times* via Getty Images

CHAPTER TEN

Waters speaks to a crowd at a rally against a GOP tax plan in 2017: Photograph by Chip Somodevilla/Getty Images

Waters protests the count of the electoral votes in the 2016 election in a joint session of Congress: © 2017, Melina Mara/*Washington Post*

Waters at the Women's Convention in October 2017: © 2017, Rachel Woolf/For the *Washington Post*

CHAPTER ELEVEN

Amen: Photograph courtesy of R. Eric Thomas

APPENDIX

Singer Mykal Kilgore performs his original song inspired by Representative Waters on *The View:* Photograph by Lou Rocco/Walt Disney Television via Getty Images

A Denver mural by Thomas Evans: Photograph courtesy of Thomas Evans

Maxine Waters–themed street art in Washington, D.C.: Photograph courtesy of R. Eric Thomas

A model rocks a Maxine Waters–themed shirt by Willy Chavarria: Photographer Brent Chua/Photograph courtesy of Willy Chavarria

A Maxine-themed Rosh Hashanah: Photograph by Doug Peck

Dr. Christina Thomas's Waters-quoting graduation cap : Photograph by Vika Jagdeo, reprinted courtesy Christina Thomas

A Maxine Waters greeting card by Etsy store This Girl's Just Sayin': Photograph courtesy Allegra Azzopardi

Eighteen-month-old Carmen as Maxine for Halloween: Photograph courtesy of Lindsay Delores Poveromo-Joly

INDEX

NOTE: *Italic* page references indicate images.

F

G

H